A Crown of Beauty for Ashes
Kathy Brown Murphy

ISBN: 979-8-234-04995-7

A CROWN OF BEAUTY FOR ASHES

Unirock Productions

Copyright March 2026

ISBN: 979-8-234-04995-7

P.O. Box 18291

Shreveport, LA 71138

Preface
A CROWN OF BEAUTY FOR ASHES

The Holy Spirit inspired me to write this healing and restoration devotional to encourage women who are going through a valley season. A valley season is a time in life one might feel alone, suffering or going through a trial. Being "in the valley" symbolically means being at a low point or trying time or a time of struggle or adversity.

Psalm 23:4: "Even though I walk through the valley of the shadow of death, I will fear no evil, for you are with me; your rod and your staff, they comfort me." Psalm 84:6: "Passing through the valley of weeping, you will find pools of blessing." This verse suggests that hardship can lead to a deeper understanding of God's grace and blessing. Isaiah 40:4-5: "Every valley shall be lifted up, every mountain and hill made low; The rugged land shall be a plain, the rough country, a broad valley." This verse speaks of a future where God will transform difficult situations and bring a sense of peace and restoration. Luke 3:5: "Every valley will be filled. Every mountain and hill will be brought low. The crooked will become straight, and the rough ways smooth." This verse, echoing Isaiah 40, promises a time of transformation where difficulties will be overcome and made smoothly. Hosea 2:15: "In that day," declares the LORD, "I will take away their names from this land; and I will call them my people, and they will call me their God." This verse speaks of God's

A CROWN OF BEAUTY FOR ASHES

ultimate promise to bring transformation and restoration to those who have suffered.

In biblical prose, "A Crown of Beauty" is a symbolic expression that indicates honor, glory and divine favor. It is often used to describe the transformation and exaltation bestowed by God upon His people. The imagery of a crown, a symbol of royalty and authority implies a state of elevated grace and splendor.

This devotional is comprised of 31 readings to motivate you to trust God's redemptive power through death, betrayal, heartbreak, suffering, loneliness, loss, and pain. After you complete the 31st day, start over as often as you need to. I speak, decree and declare wholeness in your entire life.

Isaiah 61:3…and provide for those who grieve in Zion to bestow on them a crown of beauty instead of ashes, the oil of joy instead of mourning, and a garment of praise instead of a spirit of despair. They will be called oaks of righteousness, a planting of the LORD for the display of his splendor (Isaiah 61:3).

God is going to wipe out the pain, grief, and disappointments of life and replace them with a beautiful headdress of hope and joy. In this scripture a crown is an ornate headdress that serves as a symbol of monarchy, high office, or some other position which marks its wearer as a distinguished person (encyclopedia .com).

This explains what CHRIST did for humanity. CHRIST came to restore the broken and hurting. "He heals the brokenhearted and binds up their wounds." (Psalms 147:3)

CHRIST came to provide peace, healing and wholeness for those who have been cut, wounded, and scarred by sin. The word of God reads in Psalm 8:5, He crowned you with glory (splendor), honor, and majesty that is distinctive to you. Glow your uniqueness as a demonstration of the greatness of God.

Christ died to bring out the wealth of your life as you show forth His light. The word splendor means great and impressive beauty and appearance (inside). grandeur. glory; brilliant distinction. In the sight of God, a radiant spiritual glow comes from inner qualities. Glow in your uniqueness.

Here are a few synonyms for the word splendor.
Synonyms: celebrity, renown, eminence, fame (Thesaurus .com) great brightness; brilliant light or luster. synonyms: refulgence- bright sending out rays of light, dazzle- a deep impression that affects others. You are chosen to shine! You are chosen to reflect the light of Christ and the gospel.

Oaks of righteousness is a biblical metaphor for people who live in a way that pleases God and displays his glory. The term is based on the symbolism of the oak tree as a sign of wisdom, strength, endurance, and protection. Oaks of righteousness are solidly founded in Christ and can withstand hardships(dictionary.com)

A CROWN OF BEAUTY FOR ASHES

God wants to display his power and strength on your behalf and provide for you a Crown of Beauty for Ashes. As you journey through the next 31 days, keep in mind (God can heal you everywhere you hurt). (God gives us what we need). God is a Father and will supply you with what is in alignment with your destiny and purpose. For the next 31 days surrender your will, plans, agendas, desires and ideas to God. In the Garden of Gethsemane, Jesus agonized under the pressure of the pain, darkness and despair of the cross; but for the joy set before Him he endured. The pain preceded the promise. If we are to experience the oil of joy, we will have to endure the pressing and the pressures, and will also have to die by taking up our cross daily to follow him. It is often painful to die to our own plans especially during uncertain times, however if in times of uncertainty you can endure the hardship as a good soldier, you will please the one who enlisted you. Face the challenge with strength and determination. In (Matthew 21:2-3, Mark 11:2-6, Luke 19:30-34) God instructed two disciples to go to a village nearby and untie a colt that had never been ridden. He instructed them to tell anyone who ask why, "The Master has need of it". Everything you need in this earthly life, (that pertains to life and Godliness), to fulfill your mission, God has already supplied what you need to accomplish it. Don't get distracted by what is happening in someone else's life, focus on what you need according to God's desire for you.

Do You Want to Be Made Whole?

I came to heal the brokenhearted and bind up their wounds. There are many wounded souls in the world covered with a smile. What is the soul? Your soul is your thinking, your will, and the moral or emotional nature of a human being. A wounded soul is a soul that has been injured, broken, or damaged by sin. Sins that you may have committed or sins that were committed against you.

Good news!!! God had a redemptive plan from the beginning of time because he knew that sin would enter humanity and mar his creation. The word mar means to ruin or diminish the perfection or wholeness of. The word "Made whole" means receiving full compensation for all damages, losses and other related cost.

Made whole encompasses a total restoration of mind, body, and spirit. The woman with the issue of blood was made whole by the Master. He gave her full compensation for all damages, losses and other related costs. She had instantaneous completeness.

In John 5:6, when Jesus asked the lame man if he wanted to "be made whole" (KJV), He was referring to complete restoration—physically, spiritually, and emotionally.

Jesus said in this life you may experience a storm. You may have experienced some form of brokenness—spiritual, relational, psychological, or physical; in spite of and in these times and moments the heart yet have a deep longing for complete restoration and an opportunity to be made whole again.

The Old Testament meaning of "shalom," is peace, wholeness and total wellbeing.   True wholeness is found in Christ who can heal both our visible and hidden wounds. God's work of healing extends beyond the surface. His unfailing love heals emotional scars and gives us the power to release those who have hurt us. The scars that you have is an indication that you have not been hurt beyond repair. ***According to Cleveland Clinic "A scar signifies that the body has completed the active repair phase of a wound, replacing damaged tissue with new, collagen-rich fibrous tissue. While the injury is healed, the scar itself is technically a permanent mark, though it usually matures, fades, and flattens over time."*** If the scars of your experiences are yet visible, let them be a reminder of God's healing power.   God knows that some of our struggles in life are not always a direct result of our sin, but the sin and offenses of another. His hand is the only hand that can heal the broken, but you must acknowledge that you need to be healed. Jesus can release you from the pain and control of your wounds and totally repair you inside out.

 God wants to restore you to his purpose. God wants to restore you to your blueprint potential. God wants to renew you so you will fulfill his intended role for you in the story of your life (the book about you written in Heaven). God speaks of your book in Psalm 139:16. Here's three different Bible versions that draw out God's heart about this book of yours.

A CROWN OF BEAUTY FOR ASHES

<u>The Contemporary English Version</u> says it this way, "but with Your own eyes you saw my body being formed. Even before I was born, you had written everything about me in your book.

<u>The VOICE translation</u> says it this way, "You see all things; You saw me growing, changing in my mother's womb; Every detail of my life was already written in Your book; You established the length of my life before I ever tasted the sweetness of it."

<u>The New King James Version</u> says it this way, "Your eyes saw my substance, being yet unformed. And in Your book, they all were written, the days fashioned for me, when as yet there were none of them."

The Creator's book contains your destiny, reason for being here, your work and what you have been set apart for. Everything about you, including your future, is written in it. Make sure your choices are aligned with the book of destiny your creator has written for you. Let this mind be in you that was in Christ Jesus, not my will (choice) God, but your will (choice) be done in my life.

The word purpose means the reason for which something is done, created or for which something exists. God wants to return you to the original state He intended for you. The word restore means return (someone or something) to a former condition, place, or position.

You are God's masterpiece. The word masterpiece spiritually denotes that in Christ you can do the good things He (GOD) planned for you from creation. The New Living

A CROWN OF BEAUTY FOR ASHES

Translation Ephesians 2:10 "We are GOD's masterpiece (a work of outstanding artistry and skill). HE created us anew in CHRIST JESUS, so we can do the good things He planned for us long ago. This scripture denotes that God is the ALL POWERFUL ONE who has already begun to mold you into a tapestry of strength, power, love and resilience.

God competently and artistically makes us into someone new, but not for the purpose of being seen or for personal admiration. It is for the purpose of serving others by doing good works and being spiritually fruitful that God might be glorified. If we are to display the beauty of God's design and be a representative of His work of art; it will glow through our speech, our behaviors, our relationships, our life ethics and morals. The beauty of who you are is not in the outward appearance but in the simplicity of living a fruitful life. Nothing about the outward appearance of the Acerola Cherry and other visually unappealing fruits and vegetables indicates the supercharged powerhouse benefits of what is on the inside.

Your journey to healing, restoration and multiplication begins today with understanding how much GOD loves you, but it's against his nature to force you to love Him. If you have not accepted Jesus as your Lord and Savior, accept Him today. Confess to Him that He is the only way to life and life more abundantly.

You can choose to be healed, or you can choose to remain chained in captivity to disappointments, loss, pain, and adverse experiences. If you choose to be healed and made whole, you allow the Savior and healer to embrace you and love you back to life.

He is Jehovah Rapha. Jehovah Rapha is a Hebrew phrase that means "God who heals". The word "Rapha" can also mean "to mend, to repair, or restore". Jesus came to heal your wounded soul. Do you want to be made whole?

A CROWN OF BEAUTY FOR ASHES

Day 1
Hello Beautiful Stay Connected

1 Corinthians 15:33 Don't be deceived! "Evil companionship corrupts good morals."

Get involved with the healthy and positive. How do you know if your lifestyle, involvements, and people are healthy choices.

Let's talk about it. Does it give you peace and joy? Does it provide a sense of meaning and purpose? Does it strengthen your spiritual moral values and beliefs? Does it cultivate an environment for growth and productivity? Does it enhance your overall well-being? Does it leave you emotionally drained and violated? Does it have a positive or negative effect on the management of your daily life and responsibilities? Does it bring excitement, motivation and recharge? Does it spiritually nourish your soul? Does it violate your boundaries, principles and convictions? Does it make you feel safe?   Does it lead you to God or away from God? Psalm Chapter 1 reads, Blessed is the man that walketh not in the counsel of the ungodly, nor standeth in the way of sinners, nor sitteth in the seat of the scornful. 2 But his delight is in the law of the Lord; and in his law doth he meditates day and night. 3 And he shall be like a tree planted by the rivers of water, that bringeth forth his fruit in his season; his leaf also shall not wither; and whatsoever he doeth shall prosper. 4 The ungodly are not so: but are like the chaff which the wind driveth away. 5 Therefore the ungodly shall not stand in the judgment, nor sinners in the congregation of the righteous.   6 For the Lord knoweth the way of the righteous: but the way of the ungodly shall perish.

 Be careful who you connect with and how you connect. Your eyes, ears and mouth are gateways to your soul. Associations, involvements, what you watch on TV and the music you listen to, will either weaken you or strengthen you, build you or tear you down, corrupt you or make you virtuously trustworthy, kill you or give life, destroy you or restore you, steal from you or add goodness to you.

"According to the Discourse Date of 19 February 1987 Prasanthi Nilayam Discourse Collection Sri Sathya Sai Speaks, Vol 20 (1987) The four gates to the soul are: Shama (Self-control): This requires steadfast faith in God and control of the senses and mind. It involves focusing on eternal and giving up attachments to the transient. Vicharana (Enquiry): This entails discriminating between right and wrong, good and evil, and the transient and the eternal. It's about understanding the nature of reality and the purpose of life. Tripti (Contentment): This means being satisfied with what you have, without craving for more. It's about finding joy in the present moment and recognizing the abundance that already exists. Satsangam (The company of good): This emphasizes the importance of associating with positive and virtuous individuals who can inspire and guide you on your spiritual path. It involves learning from the good and avoiding the company of the bad." End Quote

A CROWN OF BEAUTY FOR ASHES

The Bible provides us with scriptures regarding the cleansing agent of the word of God. The Bible declares that the word of God can save the soul. James 1:21 states Therefore, get rid of all moral filth and the evil that is so prevalent and humbly accept the word planted in you, which can save you. Staying connected to the right people, and the right environment is a key to healing and restoration. One way to stay connected is to get involved in life/counseling/support groups or conducive clubs. These groups can build deeper spiritual networks, build strong relationships, and provide a sympathetic community to "do life" together, supporting growth and responsibility.

Are you an intricate and active part of the Body of Christ? If not, deciding to do so, will be rewarding and life changing. Ask God to lead you to a healthy church (Christ-Faith Based Organization). What does a healthy church look like? A church that builds people. A church with consistent ethical and moral leadership. A church that does not have rivalry and competition. A church that believes in holiness and purity. A church with a spiritually protective leader. A church where leaders hold themselves and the congregation accountable for their actions. The expression "pastors don't destroy or scatter sheep" can be found in Jeremiah 23:1-6, which warns against shepherds who harm or neglect their flock, highlighting the significance of pastors caring for those whom God has entrusted into their care. The example remains significant today, as it functions as a reminder for pastors to fulfill their duties with integrity and compassion, making sure of the well-being and spiritual health of their congregations.

Avoid social isolation and loneliness. Don't be afraid to get connected!

Assignment: If you are not already connected- research opportunities available in your area.

Day 2

Hello Beautiful the Danger of Competition, Covetousness and Comparison

For am I now seeking the approval of man, or of God? Or am I trying to please man? If I were still trying to please man, I would not be a servant of Christ (Galatians 1:10, ESV).

President Theodore Roosevelt made the following quotes: *"comparison is self-defeating. Comparison is the thief of joy. A flower does not think of competing with the flower next to it. It just blooms." End quote.*   When you compare yourself to others, you destroy the uniqueness of you. God did not create you to compare yourself to others, He created you to radiate in the spirit of excellence. The word excellence means qualities to the highest degree.

The jeopardy of comparing is that our comparisons are never to our advantage, and it leads to decay. Each one of us is an exclusive and unique individual with unique life occurrences. The demands we assign to ourselves to be like those we are comparing ourselves to normally lead to feelings of reduced self-worth.

There are no two set of fingerprints that are the same. Scientific evidence proves that there are no two snowflakes that are the same. Their evolving process causes their uniqueness. As they encounter varying conditions, different paths, various temperatures, humidity levels, and even how they rotate and collide are factors that contribute to their uniqueness. Even if two snowflakes are floating side by side, they will each be blown through different levels of humidity and vapor to create a shape that is truly unique.

 Comparing yourself with someone else leads to anxiety, depression, spiritual suicide and emotional suicide. Both comparing and competition are a form of covetousness. We are provided wisdom in the Bible prohibiting covetousness. Coveting is defined as having an inordinate or excessive desire for something that belongs to another person. It's a form of envy or greed that leads to other sins.

Coveting, comparison and competition are rooted in and originate from low self-image and low self-worth. Coveting, comparison and competition results in an inner conflict and an incessant (continuous) dissatisfaction with yourself. These three culprits are not limited to material assets, they can extend to the spheres of relationships, prestige, or anything else that someone else has that you desire.

God knew you before you were formed in your mother's womb. HE has ordained your destiny and your purpose. You are not supposed to be like someone else. You are a unique detailed design. You are supposed to be content with God's design and purpose for you. Be the best version of you.   Don't use your time and energy trying to be like everyone else. Use your time and energy wisely to level up, to improve yourself, to learn, to gain wisdom and advance in life. Your primary concern should be what God Most High thinks of you and your alignment and growth in His will. Align your life with truth. Don't try to appeal to the masses. Don't lose any sleep because someone doesn't' like you. Be yourself as you are in harmony with God's word and plan.

The Bible states that Godliness with contentment is great gain. James 4:2, says, "You lust and do not have, so you murder. You covet and cannot get, so you fight and quarrel." Stop quarreling with your maker. The inner quarreling and conflict of worthiness and value results in a damaged mind. Trust that GOD has your best interest in his plan.
Trust God's sovereignty.

Being content does not mean you are not supposed to change and evolve into a higher place of notoriety and productivity. Being content does not mean you cease to work toward notable achievements. Being content means, you are embracing the present season while prayerfully preparing for the next season.   Being content means, you are at peace and harmony in your present situation because wherever you are in life, you have faith that you will grow and glow in the magnificent beauty and purpose of your CREATOR.

 Being content means that you are not looking unto others for validation and approval. Being content means you don't desire someone else's light that God has given them to shine.   Being content means you do not allow what you see in another or what others have to displace your belief in Jeremiah 29:11 "For I know the plans I have for you," declares the LORD, "plans to prosper you and not to harm you, plans to give you hope and a future." Decree it this day, "GOD has a perfect plan for me." Your responsibility is to bind your life to the word of GOD and HIS love.

To be content is a sign of spiritual maturity and trust in God's dominion, God's solution, God's methods, God's procedures, God's goodness and provision.

Ask GOD to order your steps and lead you down the path of righteousness for his name's sake. Shun comparing and competing. Glow in your distinctiveness.

Assignment: Study Exodus 20:17

Day 3

Hello Beautiful Stay Focused

Concentrate your attention and efforts on things based on importance and priority. To concentrate your efforts on what is important and what is priority you must adapt your spiritual sight that you might see clearly.

Colossians 3:2: "Set your mind on things that are above, not on things that are on earth." Hebrews 12:1-2: "Therefore, since we are surrounded by such a great cloud of witnesses, let us also lay aside every weight and the sin that clings so closely, and let us run with perseverance the race that is set before us, looking to Jesus the pioneer and perfecter of our faith..."   Psalm 101:3 reads I will not look with approval on anything that is vile. I hate what faithless people do. I will have no part in it. Romans 12:2 reads do not conform to the pattern of this world but be transformed by the renewing of your mind. Then you will be able to test and approve what God's will is- his good, pleasing and perfect will. Proverbs 4:25 says, "Let your eyes look straight ahead, and fix your gaze directly before you," emphasizing the character of the one who concentrates on the pathway of righteousness and evading distractions. You must have a focused and planned approach to life. Don't adjust your life for others to the point that it causes you to lose focus on what God has planned for you.   You must keep your eyes on your goals and not be deflected. By keeping your focus, you avoid drifting into temptation. In this verse the wisdom of Solomon emphasizes to his offspring the importance of a determined and decisive life.

 Hebrews 3:1 reads, Therefore, holy brothers and sisters, who share in the heavenly calling, fix your thoughts on Jesus, whom we acknowledge as our Apostle and High Priest. Fix your gaze (look steadily and intently, especially in admiration and thought) on spiritual goals and avoid distractions (a thing that prevents someone from giving full attention to something else).

God is giving you a loud, clear trumpeting call to action. Appreciate the value of wisdom. The wise person declines to be distracted.   Lucifer became preoccupied with what was on the other side of darkness. The phrase "looking into the dark side" is often used to denote the attraction of temptation, self-centeredness, and rebellion against law and authority. In Lucifer's case, it represents his quest of a path that turns from God's will and hugs darkness and sin.

Preoccupation with and a desire for things that are not of the light will always lead to the opposite of divine order. You must not be distracted by systems, values and operations that will separate you from God.

Eve sinned when her eyes were distracted from what God had said. She saw that the tree God had placed out-of-bounds- was "good for food, and that it was a delight to the eyes; and that the tree was to be desired to make one wise" (Genesis 3:6) states and she took some of its fruit and ate it. The spiritual lesson we learn from this account is looking with craving and longing at wrong things can divert you and keeps you from doing God's will.

The apostle John warned us that the sinful lust of the eyes as worldly, and assured us that the world is passing away, "but whoever does the will of God abides forever" (1 John 2:16–17).

1 Peter 5:8 states, be sober, be vigilant; because your adversary the devil, as a roaring lion, walketh about, seeking whom he may devour.

Assignment: Research the many forms distraction can take. List the distractions that may be preventing you from giving full attention to what is important. Ask the Holy Spirit to show you how to eliminate them from your life.

Day 4

Hello Beautiful Exercise Self-Control

As you continue your journey to healing and restoration, self-control is a crucial key. The term self-control means the ability to control oneself, in particular one's emotions and desires or the expression of them in one's behavior; especially in difficult situations or times of temptations.

Galatians 5:22-23 "But the fruit of the Spirit is love, joy, peace, patience, kindness, goodness, faithfulness, gentleness, self-control; against such things there is no law." Having self-control is a fruit of the Spirit filled life. Lack of self- control is a powerlessness to manage one's impulses, passions, and actions. Lack of self-control leads to impulsive conduct, poor decision-making and difficulty in controlling how you react. These can have a negative impact on your relationships and the well-being of your overall life.

Individuals who live a life deficient of self-control is characterized by an unstable existence dominated by the sinful nature. Lack of self-control is an indication of mental and spiritual instability.

Individuals lacking self-control normally develop unhealthy habits- which lead to an unhealthy life. They have poor money management skills, and they engage in illegal activities that lead to legal problems. Individuals with poor impulse control act without thinking. Individuals who lack self-control mentally by pass the process of thinking about the consequences of a certain behavior, thought, word, or action.

Lack of self-control is the sign of a fool. A fool does not care about his welfare. Proverbs 25:28 A man without self-control is like a city broken into and left without walls (no means of protection against the enemy). A fool sees danger but plunges in without forethought.

If you allow lack of self-control to dominate you, you can never make decisions that are in your best interest or that will be in the best interest of others. The solution is found in Galatians 5:16. Walk in spirit and you will not fulfill the lust of the flesh. What are the works of the flesh or the works of the lack of self-control? [19] Now the works of the flesh are evident, which are: [a]adultery, [b]fornication, uncleanness, lewdness, [20] idolatry, sorcery, hatred, contentions, jealousies, outbursts of wrath, selfish ambitions, dissensions, heresies, [21] envy, [c]murders, drunkenness, revelries, and the like; of which I tell you beforehand, just as I also told you in time past, that those who practice such things will not inherit the kingdom of God.

How do you walk in the spirit? Galatians 5: [24] And those who are Christ's have crucified the flesh with its passions and desires. [25] If we live in the Spirit, let us also walk in the Spirit.

Titus 2:11-12 the grace of God has appeared that offers salvation to all people. It teaches us to say "No" to ungodliness and worldly passions, and to live self-controlled, upright and godly lives in this present age.

Assignment: Make a sign that says self-control and post in locations where you are believing for victory. Example: on your refrigerator, your desk at work, your checkbook or on the door of your bedroom.

Day 5
Hello Beautiful Get Moving (Consult your
Physician)

Science proves that exercise is effective in treating
depression and depressive symptoms. Exercise is
medicine.   Exercise takes your mind off the problem.
Exercise causes the brain to switch to motivation and
positivity. Exercise builds mental and physical stamina,
producing an inner drive and resolves that quitting or
depression is not an option.

 The Bible warns us against worrying. Worrying produces
stress.   Exercise has been proven as a method to manage
stress. Exercise supports the reduction of stress hormones.
Getting involved in physical activity releases endorphins that
are called feel good endorphins- which are natural pain
killers and elevates your frame of mind.

Exercise can also serve as a mental distraction from fears
and concerns.   God did not design our bodies to be under
stress. Stress is a substantial contributor to many health
challenges.

 Cortisol and adrenaline are stress hormones. When you
start exercising with intention and consistency, your level of
cortisol and adrenaline are lowered.

 Find the time in your day to take a break from the stresses
of life. Find the time to reap the benefits of a focused and
intentional routine of physical enjoyment. It can be as
simple as a walk at the park, a visit to the gym, working in
the garden, planning intentional time for yard work,

swimming, joining an aerobics class, playing tennis, bicycling, etc.

Getting moving is what is important! Doctors will tell you that becoming active after surgery will help reduce swelling and improve blood flow, which can aid in your recovery. When you are physically wounded you must eventually become active for proper healing. When you are experiencing brokenness, you must remain active to aid in the healing process.

Exercise has many health benefits when it is coupled with positive living. Begin your exercise routine sensibly (consult your physician) according to your individual needs and health benefit.

According to empirical research, exercise is a benefit in the following ways: spurs creativity, heart health, weight management, memory and brain functions, self-efficacy, and self-esteem.

You made it to day 5. You are doing great!
Stay strong and get moving.

Assignment: Begin today with an Intentional exercise routine if you do not already have one. Pray that you remain consistent. It's always nice to have someone to exercise with. Reach out to a family member, neighbor, co-worker or friend.

Day 6

Hello Beautiful Will You Be
Bitter or Blessed

Forgiveness does not mean you have to continue to be anchored and attached to the person you forgave.

Don't grow bitter (of people or their feelings or behavior). Don't allow anger, hurt, or resentment to dominate and consume you because of your bad experiences or a sense of unjust treatment. What a person does to you or has acted toward you does not reduce your value; it reduces their value. Only you can decrease or increase your value. Let's take a closer look at the negative physical, mental, emotional, relational and spiritual effects of bitterness. Bitterness is a negative emotion. Bitterness results in hopelessness, worry, and other spiritual, physical and psychological health problems.

Bitterness erodes your personal relationships and can cause poor and neglectful performance in daily duties and responsibilities. Bitterness has the potential to diminish your sense of self care and self-worth. Bitterness has the potential to decrease your ability to enjoy life and love; and can produce a rotation of damaging thinking and negative behaviors.

Bitterness is how a person has decided to live in response to disappointment, feeling unappreciated, or a painful experience. If one chooses to embrace and hold on to the negative emotion of bitterness, that person has decided they are unworthy and don't deserve to be free of past pains. Bitterness is believing you don't have a right to be at peace. Bitterness is believing that you should live in a state of suspicion, inner conflict, and hostility. Bitterness causes a person to seek their own justice. Living in a bitter state results in low self-image.

Bitterness is choosing to live in an unforgiving frame of mind. Living bitter permits the spirit of resentment the right to forever cause you to live in pain, disappointment, cruelty, revengefulness, callousness and irritability.

Bitterness weakens proper judgements and increases the likelihood of poor decision-making abilities. Bitter people live in a trap of excuses to make poor choices.   Bitterness has the potential to convince a person that they should live in distrust and isolation because they are not comfortable being around others. Bitterness leads to the self- sabotaging of potential relationships and friendships.

Bitterness will not allow you to enjoy the life God created you to have. Decide on your freedom today. Vengeance is mine; I will repay, says the Lord" is a biblical statement from Romans 12:19, Deuteronomy 32:35. Trust God to make the wrong right. Trust God to reward and bless you for your sacrifices and restore what has been lost or stolen. Exercise self-constraint and trust God's plan instead of resorting to retaliation. Don't live wanting others to experience God's wrath. Focus on your spiritual, personal and professional growth- while trusting God's timing. Focus on the positive while you are growing through every season.

How do you combat the negative emotion of bitterness? Believe that God loves you too much to leave you alone! Believe that God got you!
It's your choice to escape the prison of needing to punish others for their actions by trying to hold them hostage in your bitterness and resentment.

If you live bitter and resentful, you are hurting and punishing yourself without relief. Show those who hurt you how to handle pain and rejection; become the best version of who God created you to be. Best means to the highest degree. Be excellent in the LORD, be outstanding in the LORD, be exemplary in the LORD. Repay evil with good.

How do you know if you have forgiven. If the person who has hurt you is hungry, you will provide food. If they are thirsty, you give them drink. If they are having an emergency, you will help them.   Let bitterness go for your own personal benefit. Let bitterness go so you can grow. A person can never give you what they do not possess. Pray for the person who hurt/offended you. Let bitterness go so you can live!

Assignment: Make a list of a situation (s) that have caused bitterness in your heart and mind.
Release it today.

Day 7

Hello Beautiful If your name is googled, what would you be known for?

Genesis 12:2   "I will make you into a great nation, and I will bless you; I will make your name great, and you will be a blessing.

New Living Translation
I will make you into a great nation. I will bless you and make you famous, and you will be a blessing to others.

Proverbs 22:1 "A good name is to be chosen rather than great riches, and favor is better than silver or gold. The word name in both verses means "reputation," "standing," or "the general estimation and recognition of a person."

In ancient Israel, a person's name was intricately linked with his or her reputation and standing in the community. The term translated "to be chosen" in the original language carries the idea of going after what is more desirable, preferable, or worth much more. The term
Favor is actually "good favor" in the original Hebrew and corresponds with name in the first line of the verse. In this framework, favor means "acceptance, respect, or esteem from other people."

A CROWN OF BEAUTY FOR ASHES

(Proverbs 21:21 Whoever pursues righteousness and love finds life, prosperity and honor.)

Titus 2:11-12- the grace of God has appeared that offers salvation to all people. It teaches us to say "No" to ungodliness and worldly passions, and to live self-controlled, upright and godly lives in this present age.

Titus 2:7-8 New International Version- In everything set them an example by doing what is good. In your teachings, you show integrity, seriousness and soundness of speech that cannot be condemned, so that those who oppose you may be ashamed because they have nothing bad to say about us.

2 Timothy 2:22 encourages one to flee youthful passions and pursue righteousness, faith, love, and peace, along with those who call on the Lord from a pure heart. You cannot regulate what others think of you, but you can live an honorable life by the power of the Holy Spirit. Only God can protect and defend your reputation, but you can guard your heart and character by guarding the gospel. If you protect the gospel, you are guarding the quality of your character.

Proverbs 4:23-27 New International Version states "Above all else, guard your heart, for everything you do flows from it. Keep your mouth free of perversity; keep corrupt talk far from your lips. Let your eyes look straight ahead; fix your gaze directly before you. Give careful thought to the paths for your feet and be steadfast in all your ways. Do not turn to the right or the left; keep your foot from evil."

The Psalmist David song "Thy word have I hid in my heart that I might not sin against God." How do you live a respectable reputable life; you do this by respecting and reverencing God. If you respect GOD and consider HIS commandments first, your choices and decisions will be moral and ethical. Esteem GOD in your decision making. The definition of esteem is to be regarded highly. Regard the HOLY one. Your creator is EL ELYON the HIGHEST. HE is the supreme sovereign authority and is in an exalted position above all creation. HE is HOLY. A new life in Christ brings newness in all things. This new life transforms you into a new person.

What are some primary things to shun to avoid reputation damage: adultery, fornication, sexual immorality, sexual impurity, lying, deceitfulness, stealing, abuse, bad company, the lust of the flesh, the lust of the eyes and the pride of life.

The lust of the flesh is any attraction or sin that draws to our carnal and physical passions. It is any sin that gives people sinful enjoyment and attempting to fulfill the emotional senses and bodily needs through sin.

The lust of the eyes is to peek at things for which we are prohibited to see. The lust of the eyes includes looking, imagining and dreaming about things God has banned us from thinking about; it is craving and thirsting to look at something or someone that you should not be gazing at.

Pride of life is the lure and desire for supremacy, power, the need to be seen and recognized. The need for personal admiration, praise and honor. The pride of life gives a person a false sense of being better because of what they might possess, who they are married to, their status in society, or their accomplishments.

Anything that is ungodly leads to a damaged reputation. Pursue what is praiseworthy.

Philippians 4:8 reads- Finally brothers and sisters, whatever is true, whatever is honorable, whatever is just, whatever is pure, whatever is lovely, whatever is commendable—if there is any moral excellence and if there is anything praiseworthy—dwell on these things. Once your character is damaged, you are no longer viewed as a person who can be trusted. Proverbs 22:1 "A good name is to be chosen rather than great riches, and favor is better than silver or gold. Your name/character should be known for sanctification, stability, reliability, and responsibility.

Assignment: google your name what do you see?

Day 8

Hello Beautiful Watch What You Eat

(Consult your Physician)

Satisfy your mouth with good things so your youth will be renewed as the eagle. Food and words have a vibrational frequency. What you ingest physically and mentally affect you spiritually and emotionally. You are what you ingest. If you want to be healthy physically and spiritually be careful what you consume. Psalm 103:5 states "Who satisfies your mouth [your necessity and desire at your personal age and situation] with good so that your youth, renewed, is like the eagle's [strong, overcoming, soaring]! God wants to fill your life with good things. The word good means morally right, positive and beneficial. Your life should be sustained first by a constant diet of the word of GOD. You cannot live (spiritually successful without it). Matthew 4:4, Jesus says, "Man shall not live by bread alone, but by every word that comes from the mouth of God. Joshua 1:8 states "Do not let the book of the LAW depart from your mouth. Mediate on it day and night then shall your way be made prosperous and you shall have good success". The word of God provides strength and direction. Just as physical food nourishes the body, the word of GOD nourishes your soul and spirit.

In John 6:63, Jesus declares that the words that HE speaks are spirt and life. The word of GOD is not just any word. The word of GOD working with the HOLY SPIRIT provides the authority to give everlasting life. The word of God changes everything about you. The word of GOD is a living active vibrational frequency. The word of GOD produces a healthy heart, a healthy attitude, a healthy spirit and a healthy mind.

Just as the word of GOD is health to our flesh according to Proverbs 4:22, the physical food we choose to consume will either produce life or death to our physical bodies. Food is the building block of life and is meant to build and repair the cells. Food is either medicine or poison. Ask yourself the following questions, what do I eat every day? Is it healing me or harming me? Am I honoring the temple of God with my food sources?   Fill your lunch box, picnic basket, refrigerator and pantry with items that will build and repair your cells. Vitality and wellness are the result of healthy eating. Spiritual vitality and wellness are the result of a healthy spiritual diet.

Consult those in the medical and dietetics and nutrition industry for empirically researched information. You can also search the scriptures. The HOLY scriptures provide purposeful dietary laws.   Educate yourself on the science of food, a balanced diet, and pray for discipline.

The following is submitted by a health and wellness expert. The beliefs and views of this article stands as an independent entry and does not necessarily reflect the beliefs of the author of this book. Enjoy reading.

<u>Through the journey of healing and restoration, it's important to also address the spiritual and emotional aspects of possible food fixations. It's very easy to run to food for comfort and satisfaction to fill the void of emptiness that can feel at times</u>

unbearable. This can also be experienced as a "starvation" or punishment of self with lack of food to show discipline and an image of self-control of the current situation.

We make food an idol when we run to it for comfort and satisfaction instead of to God. However, Psalm 94:19 says that "When my cares within me are many, your comforts cheer me up." David also shares his anguish and anxiety, and the solution in Psalms 42:12 " My soul, why are you so downcast? Why are you groaning inside me? Hope in God, since I will praise him again for being my savior and God."
(CJB)

Finally, Psalm 16:11 echoes a resounding truth of God that "You make me know the path of life; in your presence is unbounded joy, in your right-hand eternal delight."

Staying in God's presence means nourishing yourself inside and out and not fixating on punishment or unhealthy practices because of present emotions. Stay hydrated, eat when you feel hungry, take comfort in eating healthy foods, and have a sweet treat not as a reward, but as a way of mindfulness in enjoying the diversity of wonderful foods.

God's presence and his creation will continue to bring you delight, pleasure, and comfort until eternity.

Sawayla Ugwuegbu, MPH, CHES®, CWP

Owner & Chief Wellness Officer

Saloso Family Wellness

Assignment: Look in your refrigerator and cabinets, are they filled with foods that build and repair the cells?

Day 9

Hello Beautiful Separate and succeed

If you want to know where you will be three years from now look at who you are hanging around.

Let's be clear from the beginning. Separation does not mean isolation. It is about distancing yourself from the darkness. Some people are just toxic. We hear this phrase a lot. What does it really mean. It means some people are full of deadly poison. They are venomous and fatal. They will suck the life out of you. Your journey to healing and restoration and multiplication requires discarding- getting rid of- harmful Influences. Negative people and places can lead you to the pit of destruction and to the grave.

On your journey to restoration, healing and multiplication your goal is total spiritual alignment. If you are spiritually aligned with the Most High God, you will become physically aligned in all matters. This means cleaning your life of everyone and everything that is causing you to be misaligned.

Foster friendships, relationships and communion with individuals who are positive and encourages you to strengthen your foundation in Christ. Get involved with individuals who follow peace, holiness and possess an incessant desire to be victorious in Christ. Find another light to shine brightly with. Individuals who are not allied with your purpose and do not support your aspirations will eventually cause you to abandon your dreams, visions and destiny. Evil communication corrupts good morals. Evil associations will degrade your principles.

Request someone you know to be your accountability partner. Accountability partners help each other stay committed to their obligations, dreams, goals and commitments. If you are a person who loves light, you should not compromise and fellowship with darkness. The Bible reads, what fellowship does light have with darkness. The works of darkness leads to decline then ultimately death.

Engaging with individuals who love darkness leads to an unfruitful life. The works of darkness lower you and the quality of your life. A successful life is characterized by righteousness. When you separate from negative influences and cultivate a relationship with GOD, you discover your true self. Seek close connections with individuals who will help you fulfill your purpose. Walk together with them. Godly accountable partners foster compliance with the law of the LORD and discourages submitting to the distractions of the world.

  Meditate on these scriptures today.

Psalms 1:1-2 "Blessed is the man that walketh not in the counsel of the ungodly, nor standeth in the way of sinners, nor sitteth in the seat of the scornful. But his delight is in the law of the Lord; and in his law doth he meditates day and night." – Psalms 1:1-2

Philippians 4:8 "Finally, brethren, whatsoever things are true, whatsoever things are honest, whatsoever things are just, whatsoever things are pure, whatsoever things are lovely, whatsoever things are of good report; if there be any virtue, and if there be any praise, think on these things." – Philippians 4:8

1 Peter 2:9 "But ye are a chosen generation, a royal priesthood, a holy nation, a peculiar people; that ye should shew forth the praises of him who hath called you out of darkness into his marvelous light." – 1 Peter 2:9

Isaiah 35:8 "And a highway shall be there, and a way, and it shall be called the way of holiness; the unclean shall not pass over it; but it shall be for those: the wayfaring men, though fools, shall not err therein." – Isaiah 35:8

Deuteronomy 30:16 "In that I command thee this day to love the Lord thy God, to walk in his ways, and to keep his commandments and his statutes and his judgments, that thou mayest live and multiply: and the Lord thy God shall bless thee in the land whither thou goest to possess it." – Deuteronomy 30:16

Proverbs 27:17 "Iron sharpeneth iron; so, a man sharpeneth the countenance of his friend." – Proverbs 27:17

Ecclesiastes 4:12 "And if one prevails against him, two shall withstand him; and a threefold cord is not quickly broken." – Ecclesiastes 4:12

Philippians 3:20 "For our conversation is in heaven; from whence also we look for the
Saviour, the Lord Jesus Christ." – Philippians 3:20

Matthew 7 and 13 read: Enter through the narrow gate. For wide is the gate and broad is the road that leads to destruction, and many enter through it. 14 But small is the gate and narrow the road that leads to life, and only a few find it. As you continue your journey through the word of God and experience healing, restoration and multiplication, you must surround yourself with those who are marked by the same commitment.   Those whose life and conduct are in alignment with the teachings of Jesus Christ. Individuals who are willing to make the same sacrifices, live obedient to the Word of God and willing to forsake the desires of the world and the pleasures of sin. Those who have made a wholehearted decision and commitment to make the necessary changes to be ready for Christ's return for his Bride.

Assignment: create a list of individuals who are not a good spiritual influence- ask your heavenly father to save/rescue them and in the meantime begin to wisely sever the relationship with Godly love and healing.

Day 10

Hello Beautiful "The Eagle"
In continuing your journey to healing and restoration, it is necessary to study the character traits of the Eagle. The Holy scriptures provide multiple references of the eagle. In your prayer and devotion time study what the sacred writing of the Holy Bible teaches us about this majestic-extraordinary creature. Let's explore the nature and personality of this leader.

1.   The eagle has a remarkable visionary scope. The Bible tells us that without vision the people perish. The word perishes in this context can also mean without restraint. You must know God's vision for your life! You must know what your Divine Creator requires of you. Do you have children?   The Bible admonishes us to train up a child according to their life requirements and as they age, they will not depart from it.

If you do not know God's vision for your life, you will live a life that is empty, uncertain and out of control. Without vision you will live a life that lacks the quality of spiritual and personal discipline. A life without vision is characterized by uncontrolled impulsive behaviors, haphazard actions, and constantly shifting desires. When a person has vision, short or long term, he or she is intentional, precise, strategic, ignores distractions, and navigates life refusing to be sidetracked. You must be a visionary!

2.   The eagle soars with strength, power and grace. The proverbs 31 woman is not perfect, she is strong. She is graceful, she is powerful, she is the picture of resiliency, and she is adaptable. She trains her mind to soar high; for she realizes she cannot fly high living below the holy standard. Without fear she pilots critical, unpleasant, uncomfortable winds and uses them to her advantage.

3.   Like the Eagle you must live prepared. Live ready to be useful.   Be careful that you do not live to just exist. Command order in your life. Live on purpose guided by the light of destiny.   The Eagle is always prudently preparing for the future. Matthew chapter 25 gives us a parable of the five wise and five foolish virgins. The foolish virgins were

(thoughtless, silly and careless). The wise virgins were (far-sighted, practical and sensible). We all must take individual responsibility for spiritual readiness and avoid procrastination and spiritual negligence. Live in preparation for the next season.

4.	The Eagle is territorial not in a negative sense but in a positive sense. The eagle is a ferocious protector. Be a protector of justice. Be a protector of the vulnerable and weak. Speak for those who cannot protect themselves. Don't be afraid. Be bold and protect your nest (home). Protect your family and children. Society loses respect for a parent who allows children to be abused. Protect your nest spiritually and physically. Proverbs 14:1 Amplified Bible

The wise woman builds her house [on a foundation of godly precepts, and her household thrives], But the foolish one [who lacks spiritual insight] tears it down with her own hands [by ignoring godly principles]. Your home should be a place where GOD likes to visit.

5.	The eagle has the nature to adjust. Making necessary adjustments is important for survival. If you are unwilling to adjust you will not be able to advance though challenges and seasonal changes successfully.

6.	The eagle is highly clever, wise and swift. These attributes are important in daily living for precise performance and implementation.

7.	The eagle mate for life. Eagles go through a thorough testing process during their mate selections. They do not choose a mate without knowing that their companion will reflect an intense commitment to both their mate and their offspring. It is imperative to examine the integrity and capabilities of your future companion. You need to know the person you are planning to marry is fit for a lifetime of loyalty, faithfulness and commitment. When eagles mate their bond is unbroken until death; their commitment safeguard the generations. Eagles are exceptionally careful and watchful parents. They are exemplary at being master builders; their dwellings represent strength, balance and comfort.

8.   The eagle is ambitious, mentally stable, emotionally stable, sensible, reasonable, and makes good decisions, even during the storms of life. Jesus said in this life you will have tribulation or experience a storm but be of good cheer; I have overcome the storm before you experience the storm. If you are experiencing a storm or coming out of a storm, the love of Jesus will either speak to the storm or help you navigate the storm. Storms can yield a positive outcome. Storms can be used as an opportunity for growth, wisdom and maturity.   When life blows the winds of change stand firm. God has a purpose for you and if you love Him, Its working for your good. The book of Acts shares an account of Paul as a prisoner sailing to Rome. The ship encountered a storm, and everything was lost except lives. The men in charge of the ship ignored Paul's advice and their journey was filled with disaster and great loss. Because God had shown Paul a vision and given him a word, his destiny and purpose would invoke divine protection. Have you experienced a storm or are you experiencing a storm. Have faith like Paul had, he knew that everything would be alright because God's divine plan

superseded natural laws and human decisions. Just like Paul and the men on the ship had to navigate the fierce uncertain waters to make it to shore, you will make it to safety and stability also. Some of the men swam and others using broken boards, they made it shore. They made it safety. Regardless of the reason for the storm, allow it to prove the sovereignty and faithfulness of God, let it refine you and mold your character into the image of Christ.

9.   Eagles live long. They are not a prey to anything. Their high position in the food chain protects them from predation. Ephesians chapter 1 reminds us that we are seated in Heavenly places (in an exalted position) with Christ Jesus far above
all principality[a] and [b]power and [c]might and dominion, and every name that is named, not only in this age but also in that which is to come. The Bible reminds us that our life in hidden with Christ in God. In Christ you are seated above:

- Principalities- territorial, regional or jurisdictional demons
- Powers- good and evil spiritual forces. Demonic strength or influence.
- Might- strength, power, and force, both physical and spiritual
- Dominion- authority, including angelic hierarchies

10.   Eagles are courageous. Eagles are tenacious and hard working. They have an unbroken focus. You must concentrate on your goals without being distracted.

11.   Eagles are solo. By nature, eagles soar high and are independent. Eagles prefer to be alone and self-reliant. Like

the eagle, you do not need the approval and validation of others to live a purposeful life.

12.   Eagles know they are the king of their kind. Your presence should command the atmosphere. You have the majestic nature of GOD AMIGHTY living inside you. Your confidence should reflect this nature.

13.   Eagles are known to rise above the challenge in excellency. Eagles possess an exceptional balance of wisdom, good organization and focus. These are the characteristics of excellence.

The proverb 31woman is a woman of excellence. She exemplifies a complete and whole approach to life that embraces enterprise, serving her community, and family management. The Bible declares that in Daniel was an excellent spirit. Daniel 6:3 King James Version- 3 Then this Daniel was preferred above the presidents and princes, because an excellent spirit was in him; and the king thought to set him over the whole realm. What kind of person was Daniel to acquire this type of reputation? Daniel was resolute in his purpose, Daniel kept the standard high, he operated with perception, he walked in wisdom, he possessed spiritual and intellectual judgement, he was spiritually committed, he was reliable in adversity and hard conditions, he had ethics, morals, integrity and diligence.

Resolve this 10th day of your journey to take flight and be excellent.

Assignment: Create a vision board with your family.

Day 11

Hello Beautiful if you are to possess what God has for you, you must be a giant Slayer

Read 1 Samuel chapter 17

The word giant symbolizes enormous power, something or someone to be feared, unconquerable, undefeatable, unachievable, great strength, and a force to be reckoned with.

You may be facing situations that seem hopeless and insurmountable. What are you facing that seems impossible to overcome? What are you facing that seems unable to be restored or reconciled? What are you encountering that is causing you to give up? What is causing your heart to fail? What fear or situation have robbed you of your peace: Marriage and family difficulties, starting over after divorce, problems that seem to have no resolution, faith for healing, depression due to a death, passing an important exam, struggling with unforgiveness, educational challenges, financial challenges, healing from abuse, the success of a career or business venture.

As David faced goliath, you must take courage and have faith to face the giant(s) standing before you.

David did not place faith in human strength, but in the power of GOD. David called goliath uncircumcised. Circumcision was a sign of the covenant GOD made with Abraham and his descendants. This covenant meant they had a lifelong promise of God's physical and spiritual blessings.

There are blessings that you must take possession of. There are victories that must be named in your testimony, but unless you face the giants of fear and unbelief, you will not obtain what God has for you.

When some of the spies saw the giants in the land of promise, they immediately began to spread fear among the people causing doubt regarding their ability to possess the land. You will not have what God has promised you if you listen to negative fear. God knew that the children of Isreal did not have the natural strength, skills and capability to defeat giants, He only wanted them to have faith to begin the conquest. God only wanted His chosen people to trust the promise and He would do the rest. Faith without works is dead. Whatever God has assigned or required of you, have faith to begin, He will do the rest.

Back to David and Goliath. David had developed an intimate relationship with GOD during his time as a shepherd. He understood the responsibility of the shepherd. GOD was with David and David was convinced that GOD was bound to his covenant. What GOD promised HE can do.

Goliath was not a descendant of the promise. despite his size and strength, he did not have God's divine protection. David knew the LORD
OF HOST would honor HIS word for the Israelites (His chosen people). David believed in divine empowerment and

his faith triumphed over human limitations and fears. Don't be afraid to face the giants(s) standing between you and the fertile promises (plan) of God.

This narrative serves as a profound representation of the challenges and seemingly unbeatable difficulties that believers encounter in their lives. What is God requiring of you that fear is keeping you from obtaining it? What fears are mocking and taunting you today? Pick up the stones of the covenant (the word of God); declare and prophecy as David did and watch the giant(s) fall.

This is a personal testimony I would like to share. The Holy Spirit instructed me to go back to school. I graduated with my Bachelor's degree when I was Fifty-One and graduated with my Master's degree when I was Fifty- Three. After graduating, I was hired on an out of state certification and had three years to pass eight state exams to become a certified teacher in the state in which I was living. I passed all the exams except the math exam. I failed it once, and as I continued studying to re-take it, my heart began to fail with fear. I decided that after three years of being an educator, I would shift to another career. I woke up the next morning washing my face, I heard the Holy Spirit's voice as clear as any human conversation "If you don't slay the giant, you will not possess what God have for you". Immediately, I understood the message. I started diligently studying. I would go into my walk-in closet, close the door and study for hours any materials that I could find. I would only come out for necessities. I studied for eight hours a day. One evening I got an email from a friend whom I was in a study group with, she told me she had the test standard items and examples for the math tests. The book was written by a Math Professor who believed that unless a person is a math major, he/she will never pass the Math state exam requirements. I incorporated these into my study time and posted them on every wall, door and mirror. When I took both Math test, by God's grace, I passed them 10 and 13 points above the required baseline. All God wanted me to do was get started and not give up just because it seemed unobtainable.

The Philistine said to David, "Come to me, and I will give your flesh to the birds of the air and to the beasts of the field." Then David said to the Philistine, "You come to me with a sword and with a spear and with a javelin, but I come to you in the name of the LORD of hosts, the God of the armies of Israel, whom you have defied. This day the LORD will deliver you into my hand, and I will strike you down and cut off your head. And I will give the dead bodies of the host of the Philistines this day to the birds of the air and to the wild beasts of the earth, that all the earth may know that there is a God in Israel, and that all this assembly may know that the LORD saves not with sword and spear. For the battle is the LORD's, and he will give you into our hand." (1 Samuel 17:44-47)

Assignment: Write down what is tormenting you- and write down 10 scripture promises declaring victory over that area. Call a friend or family member and tell them that you are an official giant slayer.

.

Day 12

Hello Beautiful You Are Already a Bride (The Proverbs 31 Woman)

The Proverbs 31 woman is often depicted as an example of a virtuous and hardworking woman, and her character can be seen as reflecting Christ's Bride. While Proverbs 31 offers a picture of an earthly wife who shines in domestic skills and family care, it also vibrates with the idea of the Church, who is the Bride of Christ. She is defined as steady, responsible, real, extraordinary, wise, and steadfast.

Let's define the above words that characterize this beautiful lady (believer). According to Merriam Webster Dictionary Loyal- means trustworthy and reliable. **Accountable** means able to answer for one's conduct and obligations. Able to choose for oneself between right and wrong. Marked by responsibility and accountability. **Quick-witted** means having the ability to effectively and creatively deal with problems or challenges, particularly when faced with limited resources. **Clever** means the ability to perceive or infer information and to retain it as knowledge to be applied to adaptive behaviors within an environment or context. **Judicious** means to act wisely and cautiously, carefully considering the potential consequences of actions and making sensible choices to avoid unnecessary risks. **Devoted** means to be committed or fervent to a particular purpose or cause, often with a strong sense of purpose and perseverance.

As you continue your journey to healing and restoration, we can trust this perfect model to provide a guide for roles and relationships for wives, mothers, and members of the Body of Christ.

It is an honor to share the qualities of this bride. This woman is extremely dedicated to her family. She is a representation of perseverance and insight. She has a deep love for GOD.

The church (both male and female) as well as yourself is a beautiful valuable gem. Your trust, convictions, love and submission to CHRIST brands you as an admired treasure. If you have accepted Jesus as your Lord and Savior, you are already a Bride.

Food for thought: "If you never become an earthly wife, remember you are already a bride". So, live dignified and distinguished- because you have already been spoken for. You have been claimed by God and until a worthy proverbs 31 man ask your hand in holy matrimony- ask God to keep you reserved.

Assignment: Study the Proverbs 31 Woman (Bride of Christ).

Day 13

Hello Beautiful Choosing a
Spouse- Do not be
Unequally Yoked. God's
Design for marriage is True
Union not Temporary Convivence.

Proverbs 19:14 states that while "house and wealth are inherited from fathers," a "<u>prudent wife</u>" is a special gift specifically from the Lord. The Bible stresses the importance of selecting a spouse wisely, concentrating on common faith, standards, morals, and character as opposed to physical attraction, material wealth or short-lived emotions. Being married to the wrong person will suck the life out of you! Difficult relationships age you faster and can have other negative effects on you physically.

The Bible encourages believers to seek out a mate who will inspire their spiritual growth and live a life that is dedicated to Christian love and service. Marriage is never meant to be entered into due to loneliness or any self-seeking reason. Marriage is meant to be a union of purpose.

It is a blessing to find a good husband or wife. Having a good husband or wife yields many spiritual and earthy benefits. A husband or wife from the Lord adds value to your life. This is why the Bible cautions that believers should marry believers and to avoid being unequally yoked. It is necessary for the success of your marriage, family and your purpose to have the same faith and spiritual/Godly principles.

A healthy marriage involves taking one's marriage vow seriously. A healthy marriage involves love that sacrifices. A healthy marriage is an image of love and respect combined with kind-heartedness and consideration. A healthy marriage is a mature companionship.

Marriage is a profound fusion of oneness. There is a difference between bonding and fusion. A bond can break, but things that are fused together cannot be separated. Materials that are fused together indicate two or more individual objects that have been joined or merged into a single whole which cannot be divided. When objects are fused together it creates a permanent connection that is combined and no longer separate.   Read these key verses about marriage. Genesis 2:18: "It is not good that the man should be alone; I will make a helper fit for him." Proverbs 18:22: "He who finds a wife finds what is good and obtains favor from the Lord." 2 Corinthians 6:14: "Do not be unequally yoked with an unbeliever." Ephesians 5:25: "Husbands, love your wives, as Christ loved the church and gave himself up for her." Colossians 3:19: "Husbands, love your wives and do not be harsh with them." Genesis 2:24: "Therefore a man shall leave his father and his mother and hold fast to his wife, and they shall become one flesh."

Your desire to be married should not be based on carnal requirements. Marriage is a spiritual union. Marriage is a spiritual covenant.   If you struggle with low self-esteem, you will always choose a partner based on physical appearance and carnal descriptions because of your need for self-validation, external approval, and public endorsement. Individuals with healthy self-esteem choose a partner based on spiritual maturity, emotional stability, courageous vision, resiliency, resourcefulness, open mindedness (with healthy boundaries) and benevolent support. Individuals with healthy self-esteem do not care what anyone else thinks about their companion (husband or wife) because they marry for love and not social acceptance or social approval. Everything your husband needs flows from the inside of you not the outside. Even what is physically necessary flows from the inside first.

Husbands who possess healthy spirits and sound minds always speak highly about their wives. They respect them privately and publicly. A good husband or wife (spouse) doesn't inherently happen; it takes a reverent and obedient heart toward God. If an individual does not honor God, they will not honor you. If an individual does not respect God, they will not respect you. If an individual does not love God, they cannot love you.

Ponder these truths of what a healthy marriage looks like:

- Individuals possessing spiritual maturity. Spiritual maturity is living consistently in your practice of spiritual principles. Spiritually mature individuals mirror self-control, meekness, modesty, forgiveness and actions of truth and love
- Individuals who exercise true commitment to GOD
- Individuals who are truthful
- Individuals who are responsible

- Individuals who have integrity
- Individuals who have mutual respect
- Individuals who value effective communication
- Individuals who share their dreams and goals with one another

- Individuals who work together to accomplish their shared dreams and goals
- Individuals who are aligned in their beliefs about family life and their purpose
- Individuals who are transparent
- Individuals who display love through the seasons of natural changes

As you continue your journey to healing, restoration and multiplication seek GOD'S direction when choosing a spouse; pray for insight and discernment and have faith that GOD will guide your footsteps to your divinely ordained companion. **Your spouse should be a divine choice**. Believe God to connect you with your soul mate. The person who cares for your soul (core identity). Soul- the non-physical essence of who you are.

Assignment: Further research the difference between bonding and fusing. Note the importance of your findings as it relates to marriage.

Day 14
Hello Beautiful Exercise Discipline

For the next four days we will dive into the D keys necessary for achieving dreams, goals, healing and restoration. The first D is discipline. The word discipline is defined as self-control that is gained by requiring that rules or orders be obeyed, and the ability to keep working at something that is difficult.

Winners are those who make it to the finish line. Self-control is of paramount significance. Self-control is the primary requirement (to enforce what is necessary) to develop a desired behavior or attain a certain goal.

Growing up, my siblings and I would despair over what seemed to be an unachievable undertaking. My dad's reply would be "Just stick with it". This was his response when we were trying to achieve a goal that seemed hard or impossible. What you aim to accomplish may seem difficult now, but if you continue doing what it takes to attain it, you will succeed. There is something supernatural about not giving up. When you put forth natural effort, then God can add His supernatural to your natural. I believe that when God sees a person not giving up on what He has placed in them to do, He sees faith. Faith is what moves heaven and earth on your behalf.

"The first and best victory is to conquer self." ~
PLATO

"You have power over your mind—not outside events. Realize this, and you will find strength." ~ MARCUS AURELIUS

You will tread the path of success accomplishing dreams and goals when you exercise the discipline of self-restraint. On the other side of self- control, you experience Contentment, gladness, success, and fulfillment. The hard decisions that must be made to stay focused will pay off in the present and in the future. Human studies and research reported that people who have self-control are happier.

Self-discipline is the bridge between your goals stated (vision board) and your goals achieved.

Individuals who choose self- control over indulgence and gratification do not spend their time trying to make up their mind whether to engage in actions and behaviors that do not support and ally their goals, morals and values. People who choose self-control are decisive.   Individuals who exhibit and have self-control do not allow their feelings or impulses to direct their choices. They are the planners of their own actions. Self-controlled individuals take responsibility for the positive and beneficial outcomes they desire. Because of their desire to choose self-restraint, being distracted and tempted is not an option. If you live self-controlled, you will be more fruitful and have more satisfaction in life.

Jesus said if you want to be his disciple you must take up your cross daily and follow Him. A disciple in simple terms is a disciplined follower. This is a call to self-denial. Disciples of Christ- are willing to die to follow Jesus. **You are not ready to live until you are ready to die.** Dying to self is a sign of an absolute self-abandonment to God. Daily as we walk this salvation journey, it encompasses a balance of physical and spiritual discipline (self-control). Both are necessary for complete development and maturity.

According to 1 Corinthians 6:19-20 and 1 Timothy 4:8, we are admonished to be concerned for our physical bodies as a form of devotion, respect and stewardship. Spiritual discipline means engaging in practices that fosters our relationship with GOD. Meditating on the Word of God, fasting, worship, and prayer should be an important part of our daily walk. These disciplines yield righteousness and peace for those who will train their spirit and flesh to live in alignment with GOD's will and purpose.

Make discipline a priority. Develop physical and spiritual routines that will cultivate a life that pleases GOD and enable you to achieve his thoughts and plans. **When you come to the end of yourself, you come into a new beginning in God.**

Hebrews 12:11 ESV For the moment all discipline seems painful rather than pleasant, but later it yields the peaceful fruit of righteousness to those who have been trained by it.

Proverbs 12:1 ESV Whoever loves discipline loves knowledge, but he who hates reproof is stupid.

1   Corinthians 9:27 ESV But I discipline my body and keep it under control, lest after preaching to others I myself should be disqualified.

Proverbs 25:28 ESV A man without self-control is like a city broken into and left without walls.

Titus 1:8 ESV But hospitable, a lover of good, self-controlled, upright, holy, and disciplined.

2   Timothy 1:7 ESV For God gave us a spirit not of fear but of power and love and self-control.

1 Peter 4:7 ESV The end of all things is at hand; therefore, be self-controlled and sober minded for the sake of your prayers.

1 Corinthians 9:24-27 ESV Do you not know that in a race all the runners run, but only one receives the prize? So run that you may obtain it. Every athlete exercises self-control in all things. They do it to receive a perishable wreath, but we are imperishable. So, I do not run aimlessly; I do not box as one beating the air. But I discipline my body and keep it under control, lest after preaching to others I myself should be disqualified.

Proverbs 16:32 ESV Whoever is slow to anger is better than the mighty, and he who rules his spirit than he who takes a city.

Galatians 5:22-23 ESV But the fruit of the Spirit is love, joy, peace, patience, kindness, goodness, faithfulness, gentleness, self-control; against such things there is no law.

1 Corinthians 9:25 ESV Every athlete exercises self-control in all things. They do it to receive a perishable wreath, but we are imperishable.

<u>Titus 2:12</u> ESV Training us to renounce ungodliness and worldly passions, and to live self-controlled, upright, and godly lives in the present age.

Assignment: Calendar daily a physical and spiritual routine that will assist you in acquiring discipline.

Day 15
Hello Beautiful you must be Determined

For the next few days, you will have an encounter with the Ds for success. The straightforward definition of determination is refusing to give up or refusing to give in. Determination means a made-up mind. When you are determined you do not allow anyone or anything to prevent you from completing what God has ordained.   The individual who is determined refuses to tuck their tail in adversity, and they refuse to run from any diabolic plot.

A CROWN OF BEAUTY FOR ASHES

(Philippians 4:13 ESV I can do all things through him who strengthens me). There is nothing impossible with God. This scripture encourages us that though Christ we are capable of enduring when we keep our eyes on Jesus. 2 Timothy 4:7 ESV I have fought the good fight, I have finished the race, I have kept the faith. Paul is testifying that he completed his assignment and mission. You are not on this Earth by chance or accident. You are here on a mission.

 "For we are God's handiwork, created in Christ Jesus to do good works, which God prepared in advance for us to do." – Ephesians 2:10. You were born to do good works. You have a spiritual assignment, and it takes the spirt of determination in Christ to finish well done; therefore, know your assignment and don't grow weary in doing good.
Ruth knew in her heart that she was assigned to Naomi and she was determined. Ruth 1:16-18 ESV but Ruth said, "Do not urge me to leave you or to return from following you. For where you go, I will go, and where you lodge, I will lodge. Your people shall be my people, and your God my God. Where you die, I will die, and there will I be buried. May the Lord do so to me and more also if anything but death parts me from you." And when Naomi saw that she was determined to go with her, she said no more. Ruth as well as others in the scriptures provides an example of what it means to be mission oriented. Despite difficulties, stick with your assignment.

The book of Hebrews 12:1 ESV states Therefore, since we are surrounded by so great a cloud of witnesses, let us also lay aside every weight, and sin which clings so closely, and let us run with endurance the race that is set before us.

A CROWN OF BEAUTY FOR ASHES

In <u>Isaiah 50:7</u> ESV it reads But the Lord God helps me; therefore, I have not been disgraced; therefore I have set my face like a flint, and I know that I shall not be put to shame.   A flint is a very hard dark rock, it is used symbolically in the Bible to express hardness, as in the firmness of horses' hoofs. In this earthly life you will have trials that accompany a difficult task or season, you must have the hardness of resolute determination to thrive through every season.

Jesus provided for us a perfect example of resolute determination. He endured the cross, despising the shame. He finished the agonizing mission of the cross set before Him. Jesus knew he had a purpose that He must intentionally accomplish. You may have experienced a shameful, humiliating or embarrassing situation; however, be determined to set your eyes as a flint. Be determined to live out your purpose and know you have the victory over shame and adversity.

As we consider the determination of our LORD, lets reflect on the following scriptures: <u>Romans 12:11</u> ESV states do not be slothful in zeal, be fervent in spirit, serve the Lord. <u>Daniel 1:8</u> ESV reads, but Daniel resolved that he would not defile himself with the king's food, or with the wine that he drank. Therefore, he asked the chief of the eunuchs to allow him not to defile himself. Daniel settled not to defile himself even in a difficult position.

<u>Proverbs 24:10</u> ESV states If you faint in the day of adversity, your strength is small. This verse from Proverbs encourages us to remain persistent and sturdy when we face trials and

hard times. When a person is faced with difficult circumstances or barriers, it can lead to dismay and the temptation to give up. You must hate the temptation to give up. determination is vital. You must remain constant while moving forward and defeat whatever troubles come your way by holding onto confidence in the God who is able to deliver you.

Read the entire chapter of Zechariah chapter 4. <u>Zechariah 4:6</u> Then he said to me, "This is the word of the Lord to Zerubbabel: Not by might, nor by power, but by my Spirit, says the Lord of hosts. This scripture means that the ability of human cooperation and strength was needed to complete the assignment, but it would be successful by the Spirit of God. You will be victorious in completing the divine assignment God has given you only because of empowerment by His spirit.

 We are all in the construction process. God is building his Body into a Holy Priesthood. We are being developed and established. He is the potter, and we are the clay.   God is sovereign and your reliance upon the Holy one of Isreal ensure your success story despite obstacles or opposition. He gives the victory. God can guard what He has entrusted to you.   New life and strengths will be found if you refuse to be hopeless.

<u>James 1:12</u> ESV Blessed is the man who remains steadfast under trial, for when he has stood the test he will receive the crown of life, which God has promised to those who love him.

A CROWN OF BEAUTY FOR ASHES

<u>Luke 18:35-42</u> ESV

As he drew near to Jericho, a blind man was sitting by the roadside begging. And hearing a crowd going by, he inquired what this meant. They told him, "Jesus of Nazareth is passing by." And he cried out, "Jesus, Son of David, have mercy on me!" And those who were in
front rebuked him, telling him to be silent. But he cried out more, "Son of David, have mercy on me!" ...

<u>Luke 9:62</u> ESV Jesus said to him, "No one who puts his hand to the plow and looks back is fit for the kingdom of God."

Prayer

Father, sometimes giving up seems to be my only option. What I am facing seems to be an unconquerable mountain. Right now, all I can see is doomed and failure; my heart is fainting, but today I am determined to put my trust and hope in you. I leave all my questions and excuses behind. Forgive me for my non-belief. Renew my determination with relentless faith. I have put my hands to the plow, and I am determined not to look back.
In Jesus' name, I pray. Amen.

A CROWN OF BEAUTY FOR ASHES

Assignment: Write the two scriptures below and post them where necessary.

<u>Jeremiah 29:11</u> ESV

For I know the plans I have for you, declares the Lord, plans for welfare and not for evil, to give you a future and hope. Seek God through prayer for the planed purpose he has ordained for you.   If you are fulling the mission God has called you unto, witness to someone about spiritual assignments today. <u>Luke 9:62</u> ESV Jesus said to him, "No one who puts his hand to the plow and looks back is fit for the kingdom of God."

Day 16

Hello Beautiful You Must Be Dedicated

According to Cambridge Dictionary the word dedication means the willingness to give a lot of time and energy to something because it is important. Take a moment to inventory your life and daily activities. What are you dedicated to? The word important means necessary or of great value. If someone or something is valuable, you give your time and energy to it or them without hesitation. What you are passionate about, you do not neglect it. It carries the weight of necessity and value.

If you are to be dedicated to what is important, you must have the strength to say no to what is not important. How do you obtain this strength? Be dedicated to God first. Give your time and energy to what pleases God and trust Him to bring divine order to all else. When an individual is dedicated to what pleases God, what is priority in the sight of God is not a struggle.

We will take a brief peak at a few individuals mentioned in the Bible who displayed unwavering dedicated to God.

1. Joseph was dedicated to God evidenced by his dedication to Potiphar and the leadership responsibilities that was given to him.
2. Daniel was dedicated to God evidenced by his solid commitment to prayer and respect to God, even in the face of suffering.
3. Paul was dedicated to God as evidenced in his dedication in carrying the gospel and developing the Christian churches.

4. Esther's dedication to God was evidenced by her bravery to save her people from obliteration.
5. Tabitha was dedicated to God as evidenced by her attentiveness through showing charity and service to the disadvantaged in her village.

6. Timothy was dedicated to God as evidenced by his loyalty and humble submission to Paul's spiritual supervision and his charge to personal growth, maturity and devotion to the calling.
7. Caleb displayed his dedication to God exemplified in his steadfast faith in what God had promised and his bravery to claim the land that God had promised.
8. Nehemiah was determined to rebuild what had been ruined.
9. Esther was determined to go before the king that her people might be saved, even if it meant death.
10. Joshua exemplified his dedication to God as evidenced by his unyielding allegiance to lead the children of Isreal into the land God promised, as he witnessed the dedication of his leader, Moses.
11. Noah displayed his dedication to God to follow God's instruction to build the ark regardless of the mockery from those of his generation.
12. Bezalel's dedication is evident in his expert ability and leadership in constructing the tabernacle according to God's requirements. Exodus 31:2-5 "See, I have chosen Bezalel… and I have filled him with the Spirit of God, with wisdom, with understanding, with knowledge and with all kinds of skills—to make artistic designs for work in gold, silver and bronze, to cut and set stones, to work in wood,

and to engage in all kinds of crafts." Bezalel's dedication and creativeness in executing God's instructions exhibit the magnitude of utilizing one's talents and gifts for God's praise.

13. Paul was determined to make it to Rome.

14. The blind man who was told to be quiet was determined to see.

Assignment: Make a priority list titled "focus until it is done." List the things that require dedication for completion. The list should comprise of long-term goals, short-term goals and assignments.

Day 17
Hello Beautiful Are You Decisive

The word decisive means without <u>doubt</u> or <u>question</u>, and of the <u>greatest</u> importance.   Today we will study the one who was the epitome of decisiveness.

Jesus Christ demonstrated decisiveness throughout His ministry. He made definite choices in His doctrines, behavior, and greatest sacrifice. In the Garden of Gethsemane, He decisively subjected Himself to the Father's will. As He prayed, his prayer signified that He was more concerned about God's will than His will.   His definite obligation to His mission of salvation is the foundation stone of the Christian faith.

The sacred scriptures encourage believers to be decisive in their convictions and actions. In the book of James chapter 1 the church is warned of being double-minded. This chapter highlights the importance of spiritual stability.   "But when he asks, he must believe and not doubt, because he who doubts is like a wave of the sea, blown and tossed by the wind. That man should not expect to receive anything from the Lord; he is a double-minded man, unstable in all his ways."

Double mindedness is possessing two minds. Double mindedness means wavering and pulled in various directions.   Being decisive means living with one mind and that is the mind of faith and the mind of Christ.   Double mindedness leads to the inner conflict of restlessness and confusion.   The double minded person has no defined direction and as a result doesn't get anywhere. Such a person is unstable/unpredictable in all he does."

Being indecisive is like Siamese twins who are trying to walk in two directions at the same time. They cannot make any progress. If you do not have faith that God can do it, you will not make any progress.

Whatever you are believing God for, have faith. Whatever you are trying to accomplish, have faith. We make the greatest progress when we streamline our lives to God's plan. If God has given you a plan, stay with it. If God has given you a direction and a strategy, stay with it.

Proverbs chapter 3 reminds us that if we want to be decisive all we have to do is acknowledge God in all our ways and not lean on our own understanding. The Holy scriptures tell us that Jesus' sheep knows his voice. When you petition God about a thing, and you hear the voice of the Shepherd (in spiritual, personal and physical matters) follow it; don't doubt; don't question; trust and obey.

Assignment: Act with courage and conviction to bring decisiveness and stability in your life by dedicating your time, talents, gifts, efforts and finances only to what God has directed you to do.

Day 18
Hello Beautiful You Are Salt and Light

Continuing your journey to healing and restoration, it is important to live your life making a positive difference. As believers Jesus referenced us as salt and light. He explained that this is our position and responsibility in the world.

In those days salt was used as the main preservative for food. Jesus was giving his followers a lesson on their unique responsibility in being a positive agent of preservation in an evil world where ungodliness and sin have corrupted society and men. Salt was also used as a flavor enhancer. As a disciple of Christ, you are chosen to enrich and influence the world for good.

Salt also had the potential to grow stale because of impurities. If the salt was mixed with too many other minerals, it will become reduced – weakened and useless. As Christians this is the danger of allowing the values of world, lust of the flesh, the lust of the eyes, and the pride of life contaminate the pure saltiness that God desires. If you lose your identity or character of Christ, just as salt becomes useless; you risk becoming unusable also. Remember You are God's representative.

Today, we have many means of preserving food; however, in ancient times, salt was used as the main preservative. Salt was a significant and expensive commodity. When Jesus said you are the salt of the Earth, He meant that you are to add value to the world. Jesus taught his disciples that status and influence does not indicate relationship and dedication to Him, but being an agent of peace and helping others come into the knowledge of their spiritual and natural potential is a much greater indication.

 Mark 9: [50]"Salt is good, but if it loses its saltiness, how can you make it salty again? Have salt among yourselves and be at peace with each other. We are to live righteously and do good. Can you imagine the condition the world would be in if Christians lose their saltiness.

 Next, Jesus declares that you are the light of the world. Matthew 5 highlights this truth: "You are the light of the world. A city set on a hill cannot be hidden; nor does anyone light a lamp and put it under a basket, but on the lampstand, and it gives light to all who are in the house. Let your light shine before men in such a way that they may see your good works, and glorify your Father who is in heaven" (Matthew 5:14-16, NASB). God has called you out of darkness into the His marvelous light that you may be His light bearer. As you carry the torch of the Gospel of Jesus Christ and the allow the Word of God to be a lamp unto your feet and a light unto your path; you are also lighting the way for others who are in darkness.

Physical things need physical light to thrive. Humanity needs the spiritual light of Jesus to have spiritual life. John 8:12 records, "When Jesus spoke again to the people, He said, 'I am the Light of the World. Whoever follows me will never walk in darkness but have the light of life.'" Jesus is the light of the world. As the moon does not have light itself, it reflects the light of the sun; so, it is with God's people, we are to live reflecting the light of the word of God (Jesus) and the light of eternal life.

Jesus declared that if we follow Him, we will not walk in darkness, and we will refuse a life of darkness. The light of Christ in you should dispel the darkness that you encounter. Light exposes and causes hidden things to be revealed.

 It is a high calling to do the greater works that Christ said we will do because He goes the Father. You must set your affection on things above. If you set your affection on things of the Earth, your light will be blurred, and your witness will be mired.

Stay in close communion with the Light of the World. Let your light shine through the power of the Holy Spirit so that all can see it. (1 Peter 3:15) states For the gospel Light we have is not to be covered, but made obvious for all to see and benefit from, that they, too, may leave the darkness and come into the Light.

Declaration: I am salt and light everywhere I go.

Assignment: Study "Everyone Will Be Salted with Fire": Making Sense of Mark 9:49

Day 19

Hello Beautiful Beauty Is from Within

This is the day that the LORD has made, let us rejoice and be glad in it. Today we will consider the concept of true beauty. What the world considers beauty is only skin deep. The world has no idea what beauty really is. The world's concept of beauty is sinfully distorted.

I encourage you to dismiss the noise of the world and those who are governed by the principles of the world. Turn a blind eye to the world's point of view. This world is passing away with the lust thereof.

The news is filled with reports of women whom the world defines as beautiful going through divorce, rejection and shame due to adulterous-disloyal and unfaithful circumstances.

Physical appearance/attraction does not define beauty. I've heard individuals say, "she caught my eye". This is a lustful, carnal and disrespectful statement. Catching a man's eye does not make a woman valuable. Being the apple of God's eye is what makes a person truly valuable. Physical appearance is secondary to virtue, spiritual strength and resourcefulness. Those who focus on inward development will radiate with an undeniable desired glow.

Those who are influenced by the world's concept of beauty go through extreme measures to impress with their outward appearance. When you impress God, God will make impressions on your behalf. The Bible says, "It not by might nor by power but by the Spirit of God." Human effort and strength do not determine the blessings of God. Physical appearance does not determine favor. Physical appearance does not determine authenticity and worth. I must share with you the penny story that I tell women who come to me broken because of rejection. I was walking in the park one day with a dear friend who had been hurt in a relationship. While we were walking, I glanced down and saw a penny. The penny was bent, scratched, scared and thrown away. I picked up the penny and put it in my friend's hand. I asked her what is the value of the penny? She responded one cent. I then asked her what the penny looked like. She described the penny. I asked her despite what the penny looks like, does it still carry the same value? Just like that penny, you may have been abandoned, rejected, scared, scratched and bent, but you did not lose your value. Begin seeing yourself and every person you meet as a precious display of God's detailed thought and intricate masterpiece. Then and only then will you begin to value yourself and people based on their worth- from the inside not the outside.

This does not mean you are not supposed to care for the Temple of God – our bodies- it means that you are supposed to live in a manner that makes the teachings of our Lord and Savior Jesus Christ beautiful to everyone you come in contact with.

True beauty is imperishable. It extends beyond carnal definitions and descriptions. Imperishable beauty is a truth rooted in the Biblical aspect of inner spiritual qualities that surpass outward appearance. The Bible stresses the worth of inner beauty over outward factors. According to 1 Peter

3:3-4   never-ending- unfading beauty radiates from the position of the heart.

True beauty is an image of your relationship with God. This is precious in God's sight. All things that are physical will diminish over time, therefore should not be the basis which we determine value or an eternal viewpoint. The culture today prioritizes physical appearances, but God has called you to invest in spiritual growth and the development of a reputation and character that is worthy of His praise.

To the unmarried women -physical and material possessions does not Inspire true love and faithfulness.   If you desire to be married, live like you want a Proverbs 31 husband. Physical appearance does not inspire faithful and committed love. Faithful, respectful, reverent and committed love is rooted in a true connection and understanding of the purposes and plans of one's creator.

The Proverbs 31 husband does not have an immature focus. The Proverbs 31 husband is not seeking for appearance, status or possessions. The Proverbs 31 husband is seeking God for a prudent wife. Beware of individuals who choose to date and mate based on their carnal description list. Their attraction to you will soon fade. **Lust is never satisfied.**   Live to be a beautiful soul not a beautiful body. You deserve to be loved from the inside out.

The qualities of a proverb 31 husband will cause you to grow and glow. His love is deep, not superficial. Desire a mate whom you all can build your life on the perfect peace that God gives instead of the public validation from others. If you only desire to be eye candy it is false security and you will face a brutal disappointment. Resolve today that you are not eye candy, you are a soul created by God deserving of your soul mate who will love you through every season. I was listening to the radio and the commentator stated that studies indicate that we are in a lonely epidemic. Decree and declare this day that you are not desperate.

In the biblical story of Jacob, Rachel and Leah; Jacob wanted to marry Rachel because of her physical appearance. Jacob's wedding to Leah, was initially an act of trickery by Laban, her father; but it was in God's plan for the fulfillment of blessings and promises. Leah's marriage to Jacob produced the twelve sons who are the leaders of the tribes of Israel. The choice spouse that God has for you, will be a union that will produce much fruit (in all areas).

 If you live making choices from your carnal personal preferences, you always forfeit the blessing. The children of Israel desired to have a king. God told them that the king they wanted was not fit for leadership. The children of Israel were looking on the outside, but God was looking on the inside. Sure enough, Saul was a great disappointment and ultimately rejected by God due to Saul's obstinate disobedience and rejection of God's word.

Allow me a moment to share a true account of a young lady's remorse. She was dating a young man who was everything that she desired except he did not meet her physical criteria and standard. Today she is single and has given up on finding what she is looking for. She confessed that she made one of the greatest mistakes of her life by focusing on the outside instead of the inside. *The Proverbs 31 Man is just as rare as the Proverbs 31 Woman.*

A CROWN OF BEAUTY FOR ASHES

When conducting a survey of what is admired about relationships, the most popular response is when you can witness true faithful love. True love is what is admirable, not how you look or what you own.

Proclaim to the males in your family and those in your sphere of influence that God values character over appearance. Admonish them to remember that when desiring a spouse, the reason should be for the fulfillment of spiritual responsibilities and to preserve a Godly family line. The marriage union is a husband and wife who are destiny partners. They are joined together by the creator to provide each other support in reaching their highest potential. The most beautiful aspect of the marriage union is that it is designed to produce a Godly lineage.

God is never left without a witness. If you are to be married, God has a Proverbs 31 man just for you. Boaz, Hosea, Moses, and Joseph are examples of men who choose virtue and inner character over attraction. The word attraction means the feeling or liking someone especially sexually because of the way they look or behave. Lasting love is rooted in virtue. These men and countless more in today's times are taking to heart the counsel of the word of God in Proverbs chapter 31. King Lemuel's mother cautions him of the perils of choosing the wrong kind of wife. She taught him that the wrong choice in a wife would be a distraction to God's plan for his life. [10]

Who can find a truly excellent woman? One who is superior in all that she is and all that she does?

Her worth far exceeds that of rubies and expensive jewelry. [11]

She inspires trust, and her husband's heart is safe with her, and because of her, he has every good thing. 12

Every day of her life she does what is best for him, never anything harmful or hurtful. 13

Delight attends her work and guides her fingers as she selects the finest wool and flax for spinning. 14

She moves through the market like merchant ships that dock here and there in distant ports, finally arriving home with food she's carried from afar. 15

She rises from bed early, in the still of night, carefully preparing food for her family and providing a portion to her servants. 16

She has a plan. She considers some land and buys it; then with her earnings, she plants a vineyard. 17

She wraps herself in strength, carries herself with confidence, and works hard, strengthening her arms for the task at hand. 18 She tastes success and knows it is good, and under lamplight she works deep into the night. 19 Her hands skillfully place the unspun flax and wool on the distaff, and her fingers twist the spindle until thread forms. 20 She reaches out to the poor and extends mercy to those in need. 21 She is not worried about the cold or snow for her family, for she has clothed them all in warm, crimson coats. 22 She makes her own bed linens and clothes herself in purple and fine cloth. 23

Everyone recognizes her husband in the public square, and no one fails to respect him as he takes his place of leadership in the community. 24

She makes linen garments and sells them in the market, and she supplies belts for tradesmen to carry across the sea. 25

Clothed in strength and dignity, with nothing to fear,
   she smiles when she thinks about the future. 26

She conducts her conversations with wisdom, and the teaching of kindness is ever her concern. 27

She directs the activities of her household, and never does she indulge in laziness. 28

Her children rise up and bless her.

Her husband, too, joins in the praise, saying: 29

"There are some—indeed many—women who do well in every way, but of all of them only you are truly excellent." 30

Charm can be deceptive and physical beauty will not last, but a woman who reveres the Eternal should be praised above all others. 31

Celebrate all she has achieved.

Let all her accomplishments publicly praise her.[a]

Espousing the right person is one of the most focal decisions you will make; therefore, you must be selective both consciously and watchfully (prayerfully).

The Book of Proverbs concludes with an honor to a wise choice in a wife. She is strong, independent, capable, she cares for her husband, she cares for her children and she cares for the poor. The wise wife runs her household with foresight and wisdom.

"In ancient Israel, this would mean a large extended family—including servants with all their activities—and the family business. Her husband would sing her praises in public before the community leaders. Those who know her would admire her for her skillfulness, her industry, and her integrity." (Bible Gateway)

Proverbs 19:14 read: Houses and wealth are inherited from parents, but a prudent wife is from the LORD. There is a divine favor found in a Godly marriage. Proverbs 18:22 reads the expression "He who finds a wife finds a good thing and obtain favor from the LORD. It emphasizes the value of **finding (recognizing) a good wife** as a blessing from God. The word find in this scripture means recognize. A wife is not recognized externally. A wife (from the LORD) can only be recognized from within.   A good wife is seen as a friend, a companion, a partner in oneness, and a gift from God.

Marriage is a sacred institution. Marriage reflects God's design for companionship and singleness of mind and spirit, which is oneness. Marriage is not just a social institution; it is a heavenly creation. When a man finds (recognize) (spiritually discern) a good wife, it is perceived manifestation of God's favor. This **divine favor** gives blessings upon the husband and wife, launching a solid foundation for their union. When a man is blessed with a good (Godly) wife, he has received a precious gift from God Himself. Beginning today, view the term beauty from a truly biblical concept. True beauty is:

- Handling responsibilities with maturity
- Respect and reverence for GOD
- Handling adversity with grace and strength

A CROWN OF BEAUTY FOR ASHES

- Living an honorable and purposeful life
- Valuing Character
- Living a fruitful and productive life
- Valuing small and big choices
- Valuing honorable quiet habits

- Highly regarding the vulnerable and weak
- Controlling your tongue and guarding your soul, heart and mind
- Honoring God with your life and all that you possess
- Inward purity and sanctification
- Honest actions when no one is looking
- Keeping promises
- Admitting mistakes
- Showing kindness in the hard moments
- Doing what is right despite pressure or fear
- Coming back stronger after a setback
- Courage
- A kind heart and a compassionate soul
- Humility
- Being an agent of restoration and positive change
- Hope instead of despair
- Love and good works in your community and abroad
- Choosing joy and happiness
- Trust and faith in God
- Choosing peace
- Generosity with wisdom
- Gratitude
- Wisdom
- Righteous and Holy living
- Preaching and living the gospel

"For the Lord sees not as man sees man looks on the outward appearance, but the Lord looks on the heart." – 1 Samuel 16:7

"Charm is deceitful, and beauty is vain, but a woman who fears the Lord is to be praised." – Proverbs 31:30

"A gentle and quiet spirit, which in God's sight is very precious." – 1 Peter 3:4

"Let your adorning be the hidden person of the heart with the imperishable beauty of a gentle and quiet spirit." – 1 Peter 3:4

Psalm 50:2 ESV Out of Zion, the perfection of beauty, God shines forth. The beauty implied to here is not just skin-deep; it comprises grace, character, and a spiritual attraction that is noticeable by others. One's life should draw those who do not know Christ as Lord and Savior to goodness, kindness, and truth. This is the beauty that we should aspire to cultivate within.

Isaiah 62:3 ESV You shall be a crown of beauty in the hand of the Lord, and a royal diadem in the hand of your God.

 Those who preach the gospel of our Lord and Savior Jesus Christ can be described as beautiful (Rom 10:15).

Isaiah 52:7 ESV How beautiful upon the mountains are the feet of him who brings good news, who publishes peace, who brings good news of happiness, who publishes salvation, who says to Zion, "Your God reigns.

A CROWN OF BEAUTY FOR ASHES

Matthew 23:28 ESV So you also outwardly appear righteous to others, but within you are full of hypocrisy and lawlessness.

The Lord's favor is beautiful and his hopeful promises offer "beauty for ashes" for his people (Psalm 90:17 ; Isa 61:3). God is a diadem of beauty for the faithful Israelite remnant (Isa 28:5).

Isaiah 53:2 My servant grew up in the LORD's presence like a tender green shoot, like a root in dry ground. There was nothing beautiful or majestic about his appearance, nothing to attract us to him.

The Book of Revelation describes God in His undeniable majesty and splendor. We are created in His image. The concept of beauty is more important than simple attractiveness. Beauty is comparable with God's glory. The one who sits on the throne of the universe "had the appearance of jasper and a rainbow, resembling an emerald, encircled the throne" (Rev 4:3). The Holy City, the final estate prepared for God's people, is gloriously adorned as a bride for her husband (Rev 21:2)

Assignment: Study God is a diadem of beauty for the faithful Israelite remnant (Isa 28:5).

Assignment: Research what kind of man is the Proverbs 31 man.

If you are unmarried and having sexual relations, you are only a prostitute.

Day 20

Hello Beautiful Beware of The Thief

Satan is a thief

Satan works through others to kill, steal, and destroy your purpose and destiny. A thief steals, especially in secret and without using force or violence. Satan uses his servants to exploit others to get what he wants and are always watching for a way to turn a situation to profit and benefit himself, even if it damages or troubles you.

Thieves are self-seeking and have no sympathy or empathy for the people they damage. The thief wears many masks, but not for long. Their deception will eventually be exposed to all.

Thieves are opportunists and freebooters; their intent is to eternally deprive you of your value or something valuable. The motive of a thief is never pure. The Bible symbolizes a thief possessing the character of deceitfulness and destructive intentions. Thieves take what is not lawfully and principally theirs. Thieves have no respect for laws, personal or private property.

Satan and those who are working for him live a life of selfish lies. They enter your life to drain you and suck you dry. They break the standards of God's law and the law of the land for their own personal gain. These types of individuals fulfill their selfish immediate and long-term needs at the expense of others.

A CROWN OF BEAUTY FOR ASHES

The Holy scriptures advise us to watch and pray. Pray for the spirit of discernment. Observe those around you, are they allowing satan to use them? A thief is:

- Inconsiderate
- Jealous
- Unprepared

- Selfish
- Disrespectful and not ashamed to violate boundaries
- Deceitful
- A liar
- Not empathetic, feel they should be exempt from consequences of their negative behavior
- Despises your successes
- Is emotionally immature
- Seeks for opportunities to manipulate and prey on the vulnerable- the young and the weak.

Other ways to identify a thief:

- Seeks opportunities to degrade
- Desire to limit your potential and control your success
- Has a false sense of humility
- Sneaky
- Not responsible
- Not reliable
- Must be the center of attention
- Leads you away from God's will and purpose.
- Prideful
- Deceiver

- Tempter
- Opposes what is right and moral
- Corrupt nature
- Loves immorality
- Accuser
- Predator (financial and sexual)
- Convinces you that they are the only one who have your best interest at heart

Satan is on a quest to kill, steal and ultimately destroy you; don't adapt your life to his plan. 1Peter 1 5:8 - Be sober [well balanced and self-disciplined], always be alert and cautious. That enemy of yours, the devil, prowls around like a roaring lion [fiercely hungry], seeking someone to devour.

I read a testimony of a teenage girl who was raised in the LORD and had been brought up as a servant and worker in the house of GOD. She shared how she was deceived by the thief. This dear daughter's mother kept telling her husband that she was having a dream about a thief breaking into the house stealing her jewels. One day the daughter phoned the mother and told her that she was moving out of the house with a man many years older than her. He had convinced the daughter that her parents had too much control over her and did not have her best interest at heart. He was a thief that entered her life to rob her of her peace, purity and purpose, solely to fulfil his lustful desire. The daughter went through some turbulent years. The marriage ended in divorce. All her dreams and aspirations had drifted away in pain and rejection. Praise God He has restored this young lady. She went through a long journey of difficulty, because of the thief who cometh not but for to steal, kill and destroy. **Satan also uses women to destroy men. Let's also teach our sons to be spiritually alert**.

Malachi 3:17 states that you are God's treasured possession. Zechariah 9:16 reminds us of shinning like jewels in a crown. God sees you as beautiful, valuable and uniquely created. Through the Blood of Jesus, He paid a great price for you. Always remember that you are precious in the sight of God. You do not need anyone's approval to feel beautiful, precious, unique or valuable.

Zechariah 2:5 – "For I, saith the Lord, will be unto her a wall of fire round about, and will be the glory in the midst of her."

Psalm 5:12 – "For thou, Lord, wilt bless the righteous; with favor wilt thou compass him as with a shield."

Assignment: Declare God has built a hedge around me and has shielded me from the thief. Read the definitions for the words kill, steal, and destroy.

Day 21

Hello Beautiful social media can be a gateway to death, destruction and loss.

Be alert!!!!!   Social media has the potential to:

- reduce your quality of life.
- shorten the attention span.
- reduce your maturity level.

- invite the spirit of discontentment.
- reduce the quality of your personal relationships.
- reduce the quality of your relationship with GOD.
- cultivate negligence and irresponsibility.
- incite quantity (amount) over quality (excellence).
- create a pseudo (false, fake, deceptive) life.
- invite the spirit of a busybody in other people's business.
- become a platform to create a fantasy life and become the star of your show.
- decrease stability and commitment to what is honorable and pure through desiring the next new and exciting trend forsaking the good, acceptable and perfect will of God.
- be a time robber. It holds people in captivity at their own will. Be careful that your time spent on social media is not a way for you to replace a void and emptiness. Emptiness can only be filled with meaningful and purposeful activities which lead to a more fulfilling life.

The proverbs 31 Woman does not spend her time thumbing through social media platforms for she understands that her time is valuable. She realizes that social media robs and interferes with her diligence and industriousness. She evades the bread of idleness Proverbs 31:27.

The proverbs 31 woman does not utilize social media for deep emotional connections. These types of connections are surface and do not provide dept. The Proverbs 31 woman realizes that only what she does for Christ will last.

The thief of your destiny is like a roaring lion seeking whom he may devour. Be careful, he will suck the life out of you through platforms that promote competition, comparison and promised connections. Social media can be a spiritual energy of destructive, deceptive manipulation. Solid and meaningful connections can never be found via the systems of the world. Voids, emptiness, emotional and spiritual deficits will not be cured with the world's answer.

 Social media is robbing individuals of their overall confidence through constant comparison which leads to feelings of insufficiency, anxiety and a negative self-perception. Individuals who have a negative self-perception is constantly seeking approval, confirmation and validations from others.

The Bible admonishes in Proverbs chapter 3 to acknowledge God in all your ways, and He will direct your path. We are commanded not to put anything or anyone above God. When someone or something is acknowledged or respected and esteemed instead of God, an idol has been made. When you awake in the morning do you study the word of God or turn on social media? When you wake in the morning do you pray or turn on social media? When you are at work, are you being a time thief by being on social media if it is not your personal break time? When you lie down to sleep and walk by the ways, are you on social media or investing your time in spiritual matters.

Social media and other digital platforms are reducing employee effectiveness, labor quality, parental effectiveness, personal responsibility, and contributing to an increase in the divorce and infidelity rate. The more time a person spends on social media, their effectiveness is lessened.   Social media carries the potential to and for:

- adverse harmful distractions
- release unclean forces through digital gateways
- aggrievances
- discontentment
- dissatisfactions
- depression
- reduction of optimum potential
- creations of a false sense of reality.

1 Corinthians 10:23 tells us that all things are lawful, but all things are not beneficial. The New International Version states "I have the right to do anything," you say—but not everything is beneficial. "I have the right to do anything"— but not everything is constructive. The book of Romans commands the believers to yield not their members as instruments of unrighteousness.   Filter what you watch on social media and all digital platforms through the word of God. Ask yourself these questions while you are engaging in any digital/media platform/display.

- Does it edify your spirit?
- Does it build your relationship with God?
- Does it foster commitment in your personal relationships?
- Is it pure?
- Does it increase your spiritual value?
- Does it lead you towards righteousness or unrighteousness?
- Does it lead to productivity and growth?
- What spirit is being released into your life?

As a woman of God, wife or mother what habits are you forming? A habit is something that you do often and regularly, sometimes without knowing that you are doing it. A habit is an acquired behavior pattern regularly followed until it has become almost involuntary. A habit is a dominant tendency. What dominates your life? Does social media dominate your life. A habit is a routine of behavior that is repeated regularly and tends to occur subconsciously.   Will the routines and behaviors that you are forming daily produce good success?

Be careful of the negative effects of the excessive use of social media, digital communications, and virtual interactions; which can lead to unfaithfulness, negligence and addiction.

 Behavioral patterns that humans repeat become imprinted in <u>neural pathways</u> in the brain.   Social media and digital platforms can trigger dopamine and create addiction pathways in the brain. Here are a couple of definitions for addiction. Addiction is a chronic brain disorder that involves compulsive seeking and taking of a substance or performing of an activity or behavior despite negative or harmful consequences.   Addiction is a chronic brain dysfunction that involves reward, motivation, and memory. negative addictions lead to negative outcomes, which will reduce your quality of life. **Always keep in mind what you do on a daily basis becomes a habit. Whatever you can't say no to is what you are a slave to.**

 As a Bride of Christ, you are called and expected to be intentional in every aspect of your life.   When you are intentional you plan your life and activities wisely. Planning wisely leads to ongoing positive productivity and accomplishment.

Assignment: Start tracking the amount of time you spend on social media. Declare that every gateway of communication is sanctified in your life and in the life of your loved ones.

Day 22

Hello Beautiful Exercise Prudence

Proverbs 22:3 The prudent sees evil and hides himself, But the naïve(simple-childish) go on, and are punished for it.

Prudence is at the core of wisdom, good judgement and discretion. Discernment, self-control, foresight, and sound thinking are important concepts of prudence according to the Holy Scriptures. **The word "prudence" comes from the Latin word "prudentia" which means "seeing ahead, sagacity, foresight." It refers to the ability to rule and discipline yourself using sound reasoning. The prudent is enabled by forethought to distinguish good from evil in any given condition and choose the good (Bible Dictionary).**

Prudence has a close connection to wisdom. Prudence is the application of knowledge and wisdom in situations that will provide individuals with the best path of action to take.

Prudence enables you to be thoughtful and cautious while avoiding excesses. Proverbs 8:12 states: "I, wisdom, dwell together with prudence." Prudence enables you to apply wisdom in daily life. Wisdom is the desire to be able to understand the divine ways of God Almighty.

On your journey to healing, restoration and multiplication, having wisdom in practical matters are paramount. In every season of life, you will have crossroads. When you arrive at these crossroads, it is crucial that you carefully consider various alternatives and pursue the option which is most likely to result in positive long-term effects. By doing this you are carefully planning for the present and the upcoming season.

In 1 Kings chapter 3 and 2 Chronicles chapter 1, the Bible records that God ask King Solomon to let his request for anything be made known. Solomon asked God for wisdom and understanding to rule in a just manner. Because of Solomon's unselfish heart, God gave him the blessing of wisdom, riches and honor. Proverbs 3:16 reads – Long life is in her (wisdom) right hand, in her left hand are riches and honor. Wisdom yields a long, prosperous and blessed life. Proverbs 4:7 indicates that wisdom should be our primary desire. Having wisdom and understanding should be above all else. "Wisdom is the principal thing" Proverbs 4:7, meaning wisdom is the most critical, primary, and treasured benefit one can obtain. Wisdom with knowledgeable application should be desired more than wealth, status or education. If you live wise it will bring honor, favor, and true success. Let wisdom guide your decisions.

A prudent person demonstrates sound judgement in the way they act and the way they talk. Prudent people are moderate. They are fair evaluators. They do not allow charm or hatred to deter them from making wise choices. The prudent person lives mindful balancing and exercising control over desires and passions that will destroy their future.

Proverbs 14:15 states, "The simple believe anything, but the prudent give thought to their steps." Prudence leads to self-control and moderation. Healing, restoration and multiplication involve avoiding decisions based on impulse and feelings. Reckless decisions cause hurt and damage. Prudence and careful thought lead to life and positive consequences.

 Proverbs 13:16 notes that "all who are prudent act with knowledge, but fools expose their folly." Prudent people prayerfully inquire of God's wisdom when making crucial decisions in areas like relationships, careers, finances, etc. Colossians 4:5 counsels us to walk wisely and make the best use of time and opportunities. As you are experiencing restoration, healing and multiplication, foster the virtue of prudence. Walk well-intentioned - not negligent. Live daily reflecting and making self-awareness observations that will raise your mindfulness and attention to the ways of prudence.

Assignment: Take an inventory of your life- Journal how you can make wiser choices and decisions.

Day 23
Hello Beautiful -Trust

Today I had the privilege of babysitting my great nephew. The lesson the Holy Spirit retaught me was trust. As I carefully and attentively watched him so he would not hurt himself, guarded him from harm and dangers, fed him, and changed soiled diapers; Holy Spirit reminded me this is how I should trust God. God is omniscience, omnipotent and omnipresent.

- Psalm 121:3 "He will not let you stumble; the one who watches over you will not slumber."
- Psalm 37:23 "The Lord directs the steps of the godly. He delights in every detail of their lives."
- Psalm 33:18-19 ESV Behold, the eye of the LORD is on those who fear him, on those who hope in his steadfast love, that he may deliver their soul from death and keep them alive in famine.

My nephew had no care for anything; he crawled and played without anxiety. He did not worry if I would take measures to protect him, feed him when he was hungry and change his diaper when it was soiled. He did not have any fears of care.

The Psalmist song, "I will trust in God's unfailing love". Have faith in God and you will have good success in every area of your life. In Joshua chapter 1 we are reminded that as we do not let the Book of the law (Bible) depart from our mouth, we will have good success. Faith cometh by hearing and hearing by the Word of God. Psalm 91 tells us that God will give his angels charge over us to keep us in all our ways. The expression give charge over in <u>Psalm 91:11</u> is a version of a Hebrew verb meaning "to command, give an order, or charge someone to do something." Angels are spiritual beings who are God's assistance. One responsibility assigned to <u>angels</u> is to carry out God's sovereign protection over humanity. Angels are celestial beings assigned with the duty of watching over, safe-guarding and defending God's people. In all thy ways covers every aspect of your life. God's angelic protectors protect you from physical, emotional or spiritual damages. Angels provide invisible guards to prevent harm and guide you towards safety.   They are not only messengers but also guardians, intervening in human affairs to defend and guide. In Acts chapter 27, Paul and the men were shipwrecked, made it to shore on broken planks. They made it on broken boards, but they made it.   You may be in a situation where you feel you are on a broken board, barely hanging on, trust God, you are on your way to the shore of safety, peace and restoration. In Psalm chapter 91, The NL translation states, "For he will order his angels to protect you wherever you go." The New International translation reads, "For he will command his angels concerning you to guard you in all your ways." God is the One commanding protection; the angels are simply His representatives to carry out God's orders. This Psalm reflects the humility and simple trust of the person who places their full confidence in God. Let your faith be anchored in God's power. This kind of trust is void of pride, desire and worry. This confidence is a calm and quiet dependence on God's care.

Trust God as a child trust a loving parent or caregiver.

"So do not fear, for I am with you; do not be dismayed, for I am your God. I will strengthen you and help you; I will uphold you with my righteous right hand." – Isaiah 41:10

"Those who know your name trust in you, for you, Lord, have never forsaken those who seek you." – Psalms 9:10

"It is better to take refuge in the Lord than to trust in humans." – Psalms 118:8

"When I am afraid, I put my trust in you." – Psalms 56:3

"Whether you turn to the right or to the left, your ears will hear a voice behind you, saying, 'This is the way; walk in it.'" – Isaiah 30:21

"I will instruct you and teach you in the way you should go; I will counsel you with my loving eye on you." – Psalms 32:8"

Do not be anxious about anything, but in every situation, by prayer and petition, with thanksgiving, present your requests to God. And the peace of God, which transcends all understanding, will guard your hearts and your minds in Christ Jesus." – Philippians 4:6-7

"I sought the Lord, and He answered me; he delivered me from all my fears." – Psalms 34:4

"He holds success in store for the upright; He is a shield to those whose walk is blameless." – Proverbs 2:7

"The Lord is my strength and my shield; my heart trusts in Him, and He helps me. My heart leaps for joy, and with my song I praise Him." – Psalms 28:7

Assignment: What is the meaning of God will counsel you with His loving eye on you in Psalm 32:8

Day 24
Hello Beautiful-Elijah Prayed Seven Times

Seven (7) - God will complete what He started

According to the Torah.com, numbers in Biblical times were often representational of a more meaningful implication and significance. The number seven is especially important in the Bible, appearing over 700 times. From the seven days of Creation to the many "sevens" in Revelation; the number seven indicates ideas such as completion, perfection, exoneration, healing, and the fulfillment of promises and oaths. Jesus spoke seven phrases before commending his spirit to God. The Lord's prayer is comprised of seven pleas. Jesus used seven descriptions to describe himself. King David referenced the number seven in explaining the perfect nature of God's words when he wrote that the Lord's words are flawless, "like gold refined seven times" (Psalm 12:6). Likewise, when the prophet Isaiah portrayed the coming Messiah, he listed seven qualities that the Savior would symbolize (Isaiah 11:1-2). The Israelites were to cancel all debt every seven years. Jesus commanded us to forgive seven times seventy. Naman the leper bathed seven times in the Jordan River and was healed. The children of Isreal marched around the Jerico wall seven times.   The number seven is mentioned in the Bible over 700 times.

According to the Torah.com, the number seven also recurrently accompanies fulfilling promises or oaths. The Hebrew word for swearing an oath (shaba) and the Hebrew word for seven (sheba) both derive from the Hebrew word meaning satisfaction or fullness (saba). God promised to never flood the Earth again with water. This was an oath in the sign of a rainbow. The rainbow has seven colors. In the Bible oaths would often be sworn with gifts of seven. Abraham performed an oath at "Beersheba," which interchangeably means "well of the oath" or "well of seven." The book of Revelations uses groupings of seven to represent the fulfillment of the divine promise.

 In 1 Kings chapter 18 God told Elijah to go and present himself to Ahab and it would rain again upon the Earth. Elijah did as God directed (read 1 Kings chapter 18).   Elijah prayed but nothing manifested until after the seventh time. After the seventh time, his servant saw a cloud about the size of a man's hand.   Elijah showed persistence in prayer. Elijah trusted God's sovereignty. Elijah believed that God would fulfill His promise/oath. Elijah knew that if God spoke it, it would come to existence.

Elijah positioned himself for divine acceleration and a rapid release and manifestation of God's word. Elijah expected an answer, and he would not cease praying (reminding God of His oath) until he saw the answer manifest. I believe that Elijah worshiped God and reminded God of His word every time he prayed.

Since writing this day's devotional, I have started intentionally worshiping and praying seven times per day, fasting from 7pm to 7am and during extended fasting periods, I fast in seven days increments (with the counsel of a physician). I am witnessing the divine hand of God in my life in a deeper and more miraculous way.   I set my alarm clock as a reminder to pray.

Beginning today, embed faithful persistent prayer as a part of your daily routine and lifestyle. Persistence in prayer produces perfection, exoneration, completion and healing.

Let's define these terms which will enlighten a deeper understanding of this concept:

Perfection: a state of completeness or absolute wholeness. Biblical perfection implicates freedom from fault, defect, or shortcoming. In the New Testament, a Greek term for "perfection" can also mean "maturity."

Exoneration: free from an accusation.

Completion: the idea of being whole, lacking nothing, and fully equipped for a purpose. The Greek word "teleios" (τέλειος) is frequently translated as "perfect" or "mature," suggesting a state of spiritual maturity and readiness.

Healing: The biblical meaning of healing extends beyond physical ailments; it encompasses emotional and spiritual dimensions as well. Healing signifies the restoration of one's relationship with God and others. It reflects the promise that God cares for our well-being in every aspect of life.

God has promised you all these.

Assignment: Search the scriptures for number seven. Search the scriptures on prayer.   Conduct your own personal Bible study on those who were persistent in prayer.

Day 25
Hello Beautiful Invest in yourself

Invest means putting time or energy into something aiming to become better or more successful. As you continue your journey to restoration and healing and multiplication, progress and improvement is a huge part of having a

spiritually rich life. It is **OK** to put some time and effort into yourself and your purpose. When the Bible speaks of a spiritually rich life, it is not rich in the sense of money and possessions, but rich in the things that money can't purchase. If you want to be rich in the things that money cannot buy, it begins with putting time and energy into you as a person and God's plan for your life. Some investments will require self-denial, sacrifice and an abandonment of your comfort zone.   If you desire to have a better life, don't expect anyone else to make the sacrifice for you. You must determine to make the sacrifice to better yourself. Investing in yourself increases your value and worth.   How do you invest in yourself?   Today we will identify some simple ways to invest in yourself and your purpose through self-care and a growth mindset.

- embed the discipline of prayer, fasting and reading God's word into your daily routine
- take a stroll or walk.
- Join an exercise group
- have lunch with a friend
- choose eating habits that will increase your strength and vitality

- you may consider joining a Christian women's counseling/prayer group or organization for additional support if you are facing a challenging situation
- continue your education

- get involved in platforms that will increase your knowledge
- enhance your skills and abilities
- stay on the cutting edge
- use some of your free time to engage in hobbies
- start a business- use your skills, gifts, and special abilities
- research organizations that need volunteers
- use your gifts and talents to help others and to grow your income
- make spa day a habit (even if your spa day is in your own bathroom)
- make personal care appointments a regular routine
- buy yourself something every pay period- It does not have to be an expensive purchase- something that adds meaning and progress to your life
- request help when you need it
- play and listen to soft stress relieving music
- don't compare yourself and your life with others- live according to God's will for you. Invest in His plan for you
- attend personal growth events
- prioritize getting sufficient rest
- realize it's ok to say "No". Recognize what and who is wasting your time

- recognize what is valuable and beneficial in your life.
- have an appreciative attitude
- take simple mini vacations and getaways as often as you can
- do something nice and thoughtful for someone daily ECT!

Isaiah 58:11 "The Lord will guide you always; He will satisfy your needs in a sun-scorched land and will strengthen your frame. You will be like a well-watered garden, like a spring whose waters never fail." **Investing in yourself does not grant permission to neglect your family or other required responsibilities. Balance is a necessity. If balance is lacking, self-care turns into selfishness**. Investing in yourself is fundamental for your spiritual and psychological health and prosperity. Helping yourself helps you to be able to help others. "Helping myself so I can help others" should be the reason for self-care. We are called to serve others, but you can't effectively serve others if you do not devote some time to yourself. Jesus himself made it a habit to depart for some alone time. Investing in yourself spiritually and physically keeps you positively marketable in this life and a beneficial asset in the Kingdom of God.

Assignment: For the next seven days write down on your calendar what you did to invest in yourself. What was the result? How did it help you to become better or more successful? How did you become more of the person you dream of being? Google scriptures about being a helper.

Day 26
Hello Beautiful Lay It aside

Hebrews 12:1

In Hebrews 12:1, the word "weight" refers to impediments or burdens that hamper one's spiritual advancement and ability to effectively run the race of faith. It is placed in the same sentence with sin, which is defined as an upsetting and difficult habit that easily ensnares believers. The verse admonishes Christians to lay aside these weights and sins if they are to run with resolution in their conviction simultaneously focusing on their relationship with Jesus.

A weight is an encumbrance. In real estate an encumbrance is defined as a limitation, liability or restriction that restricts how an owner can utilize their property. Encumbrances can have a brutally negative impact on a property 's value. They have great potential to decrease value and cause delays or terminations when selling a property. Encumbrances can also affect a property's transferability.

The word weight is a verb to describe the removal of clothes as the Greeks would compete with as less clothes as possible. This scripture admonishes the believer to lay aside all hindrances that will keep him or her from getting to the finish line victoriously.

Ask the Holy Spirit to help you identify weights-encumbrances that may exist in your life. The road to healing, restoration and multiplication involves being transparent and leaving nothing hidden. Honestly take an inventory of your life. Ask God to open your eyes to the truth. What are some things, activities or people who may be hindering your effectiveness? What or who may be having a negative impact on your life that is causing your value to decrease? What activity or involvement is possibly causing an impediment or restriction on your optimal usefulness for the kingdom of God?

Weights may not be necessarily sin, but they lead to and open the door to sin. Weights impede spiritual growth and maturity.

Let's explore the word besetting. The word besetting according to Merriam Webster Dictionary means constantly present or attacking.

Besetting sin in the Bible denotes habitual actions, patterns, or attitudes that constantly entangle individuals and hinder spiritual maturity and growth. These ongoing failings causes one to feel imprisoned in a cycle of guilt or defeat. Hebrews 12:1 reads

"Therefore, since we are surrounded by such a great cloud of witnesses, let us throw off every encumbrance and the sin that so easily entangles, and let us run with endurance the race set out for us." In this passage, the phrase "the sin that so easily entangles" defines a sin that seems to grip and battle every effort to overcome it. Besetting sins are not inconsequential slip-ups or insignificant weaknesses. Besetting sins are extremely deep-rooted behaviors and mentalities that oppose the conversion Christ intends for every believer.

You do not have to allow besetting sins to control you. Here are some scriptures that prove that Christ's sacrifice gave us freedom from living a life of sin.   In Christ, we have been set free from our sins and are no longer slaves to sin (John 8:36). We are dead to sin: "I have been crucified with Christ, and I no longer live, but Christ lives in me. The life I now live in the body, I live by faith in the Son of God, who loved me and gave himself for me" (Galatians 2:20).

Consider these spiritual recommendations as you lay aside "the sin that so easily entangles" (Hebrews 12:1). Keep away tempting situations and relationships, making "no provision for the flesh" (Romans 13:14, NKJV). Pray for wisdom, strength and courage to break spiritual and natural deadly habits. Marinate yourself in the Word of God (Psalm 1:1–2; John 17:17).

When we come to the true eye-opening realization that all things that are hidden will be revealed, we will begin to stop hiding our sins and face the necessary reality of change. If you want restoration, healing and multiplication, you must ask God to turn the search light from heaven on your soul and if He finds anything that should not be, take it out and save (rescue) you. Tell God today that you want to live right, spiritually focused and holy.

Assignment: Make a of List the weights/encumbrances and sin that entangles you. Strip them off/ Lay them aside

Day 27
Hello Beautiful Build A Strong Foundation

When construction companies build homes and buildings, they will tell you that the foundation is critical. The foundation is the base that supports and protects the entire structure. When building any structure, if the foundation is not strong the structure will:

- lack stability
- eventually have cracks
- eventually have water damage
- have problems with insulation
- Problems with uneven settling

All these will cause the structure to potentially collapse. Let's deep dive into verses in the Bible that emphasize the importance of a strong foundation especially in our lives and faith. In Matthew chapter seven we are provided with an important illustration of the wise and foolish builder. This illustration teaches us that the stability of one's life is determined on what a person builds on. Building your life on the teachings of Jesus and the word of God is supreme. Building on the foundation of Jesus, you will not be put to shame.

The teachings of Jesus and the principles of the word of God are quality materials to build a foundation. The Bible tells us that we are in this world but not of the world. The unwise builders build foundations on superficial carnal materials, worldly concepts and worldly ideas. These materials provide a weak temporary foundation. Individuals who build their lives on these things are just going through the motion. Going through the motions means carrying out a duty or activity without genuine interest, excitement, or commitment. What are you involved in that has become a motionless routine or a motionless requirement? Motionless infers acting mechanically and detached; simply doing what is expected without real feeling or passion behind it.

The spiritual materials from heaven are faith, faithfulness and genuine love.

 Psalm 127:1 reads unless the LORD builds the house (spiritual house and physical house) they labor in vain that build. God must be the center of every area of your life. God must be the motive for all that you do.   Ephesians 2:20 states that Jesus Christ is the firm foundation. The purpose of the foundation is to bear the weight and the pressure of the entire house. If Jesus is not the foundation of what you are building, structural damage, failure and collapse is inevitable.

Your physical house, your spiritual house, relationships, business and involvements that are built on the Rock (Jesus) withstands storms and trials, but what is built on worldly concepts is already weak and destroyed.

As a former Real Estate Agent, I was taught that a home with a stable foundation is more attractive to buyers and has a higher market value. If you build your life on the foundation of Jesus Christ, it increases your spiritual and natural value.

The Bible tells us that a tree is known by the fruit it bears. Individuals with foundation issues are unsafe and not trustworthy. Surround yourself with safe, responsible, supportive people who have your total best interest at heart. This does not mean that we cast away certain individuals who need the great physician (Jesus), it means that you care enough for yourself and them to be an advocate of spiritual wholeness. We do not cast away those who need the great physician, but we are to protect ourselves from the contamination of sin, wasted effort, and time thieves.

If you or someone you know have foundation issues, don't be afraid to address them with promptness and wisdom to prevent:

- Loss
- Repeated negative cycles and patterns
- Failure and collapse
- Irreparable damages and costly repairs.

Assignment: Read the following verses

- Matthew 7:24-27

- 1 Corinthians 3:10-11

- Ephesians 2:20-22

- Isaiah 28:16

- Psalm 127:1

Day 28
Hello Beautiful Live Unoffended and Turn Your Attention Towards Inner Peace, Love and Unity

According to Merriam Webster Dictionary here is a list of synonyms for the word offense:

- Hurt
- Displeasure
- Resentment- lasting indignation or ill will
- Huff- an emotional response to or an emotional state resulting from a slight or indignity

An offended person lives in feelings of wounded self-importance, arrogance and pride. These are the fruits of unforgiveness.   Living in a wounded, resentful and bitter state of heart results in hostility and anger.   Hostility and anger lead to destruction.

We all have been offended in some way or the other. **Hurt people hurt people. Until a person is healed from their own issues of pain and offense, the manner in which they treat you will flow from their unhealed issues.**

Be careful how you deal with pain and offenses. As humans we do anything and everything to avoid pain- even wrong things.   Resolve today to handle pain and offenses God's way. John 20:23 states If you might forgive the sins of any, they are forgiven them; if you might retain any, they are retained.   Where are these sins retained? In the person who refuses to forgive. The same sin you refuse to forgive will manifest in you and your off spring. The Holy Scriptures teach us the danger of living offended and the vitality that accompanies forgiveness.

Ask the Holy Spirit to teach you how to navigate the dynamics of a difficult relationship. There are some people who will refuse to be converted. These individuals are living in a reprobated state of mind. According to Wettstein's interpretation, they have "an unfit mind, incapable of properly performing its function of moral discrimination. They refused to have God in their knowledge and "God gives them up to a reprobate -unacknowledged mind." People who are void of understanding have a spiritual emptiness that blocks and prohibit the ability to fully appreciate or engage with deeper faith-related insights. Some people have a seared conscious. A seared conscious is a conscious position of diminished ethical senses. A seared conscious is one that has been hardened and closed due to consistent sin, indifference, or rejecting truth. A seared conscious is identified by loss of admitting to wrongdoing, loss of deep regret for a wrong committed, or moral offenses. A seared conscious will always justify wrongdoing.

Don't allow unhealed-reprobate people block your blessings. Individuals who refuse healing will drain your strength, energy and resources. They will deplete your vitality.

- They are not growing so they do not want you to grow.
- They are unfaithful and they want you to be unfaithful.
- They are unfruitful, so they want you to be unfruitful.

- They have built their lives on lies and deceit and they want you to join them in living a deceitful lie.
- They are in bondage, and they want you to be in bondage.
- They are not developing so they do not want you to develop.
- They are not happy, so they do not want you to be happy.
- They are not at peace, so they do not want you to be at peace.
- They are not successful, so they do not want you to be successful.
- They are not married, so they do not want you to be married.
- They are not favored, so they do not want you to be favored.
- They are not free, so they do not want you to be free.
- They are not content, so they do not want you to be content.
- They are not blessed, so they do not want you to be blessed.
- They are not obedient, so they do not want you to be obedient.
- They are in a spiritual and mental pit, so they want you to be in a spiritual and mental pit.
- They love sin and they want you to love sin.
- They are divorced and they want you to be divorced.
- Their life is out of control, and they want your life to be out of control.
- They have made bad choices all their lives and they want you to suffer the consequences with them.

- They are miserable and they want you to be miserable.
- They are double minded, and they want you to be double minded. They are unstable and they want you to be unstable.
- They have no intention of doing right and they want to drag you to hell with them.
- They are not sold out for Jesus, and they want you to live a superficial religious life.

Reprobate also means that which is rejected on account of its own worthlessness. This word is also used with reference to people cast away or denied and unwanted because they have failed to make use of opportunities offered them.

Don't live offended because of the actions of others. Pray for them that their blind eyes and mind will be open to truth. Forgiving others helps you to live a balanced and fruitful life. Holding on to offenses is self-poisoning and causes one's spiritual growth to be hindered.

Forgiveness leads to the path to healing, reconciliation, restoration and multiplication. Vengeance is mine saith the LORD, I will repay. This verse does not mean that God is keeping a checklist of retaliation against those who hurt you, it means that He will bless you in a phenomenal way. He will prepare a table before you in the presence of your enemies.

Releasing those who hurt you frees you from bondage. Releasing those who offended you allows you to live in joy, peace, and contentment. You must see people as God sees them. The person who hurt or offended you is a soul. Their soul will spend eternity somewhere. They need know their victory in Christ. Let the Light of Christ shine through you. Read the following verses that inspires the disciplined follower of Christ to forgive others and turn their attention towards inner peace, love and unity.

- Proverbs 19:11: "A man's wisdom gives him patience; it is to his glory to overlook an offense."

- Proverbs 18:19: "A brother offended is harder to be won than a strong city, and contentions are like the bars of a castle."

- 1 Corinthians 13:5: "Love ... is not easily provoked, thinks no evil."

- Matthew 11:6: "And blessed is the one who is not offended by me."

- Luke 6:22-23: "Blessed are you when people hate you, when they exclude you and insult you and reject your name as evil, because of the Son of Man. Rejoice in that day and leap for joy, because great is your reward in heaven. For that is how their ancestors treated the prophets."

- Matthew 6:14-15: "For if you forgive other people when they sin against you, your heavenly Father will also forgive you. But if you do not forgive others their sins, your Father will not forgive your sins."

- <u>Colossians 3:13</u>: "Bear with each other and forgive one another if any of you have a grievance against someone. Forgive as the Lord forgave you."

- <u>1 Peter 4:8</u>: "Above all, love each other deeply, because love covers over a multitude of sins."

- <u>Ephesians 4:31-32</u>: "Get rid of all bitterness, rage and anger, brawling and slander, along with every form of malice. Be kind and compassionate to one another, forgiving each other, just as in Christ God forgave you."

- <u>Matthew 5:23-24</u>: Jesus warns the believer to reconcile with a brother before offering gifts to God.

- <u>Luke 17:3-4</u>: Jesus teaches about forgiving a brother who sins against you seven times a day if they repent.

When you hold on to offenses you cease to live. Unforgiveness kills everything inside you and around you. When others act in ways that cause hurt, agitation, and aggravations; you should choose to be psychologically mature and courageous to respond with grace. Responding with grace does not mean that you accept negative behavior; it means that you refuse to take it personal and you refuse to be controlled by the emotional and spiritual immaturity of others.

Jesus lived unoffended. He did not take assaults and insults personally. He knew his worth, destiny and mission. He did not allow His enemies to sidetrack Him or provoke Him to unacceptable actions and behaviors.

Assignment: Self reflect- write down the names of those whom you are holding in an offense. Remember unforgiveness holds you in bondage. Pray for them, forgive them and release yourself.

Day 29

Hello Beautiful Be A Good Steward

Luke 16:10
"One who is faithful in a very little is also faithful in much, and one who is dishonest in very little is also dishonest in much.

A steward is an administrator, a manager, or supervisor. The word steward in the Bible means a manager of a household. Being a good steward encompasses managing: time, talents, family/ work responsibilities and possessions. You are also required to be a good steward of your personal relationships and those whom God has placed in your sphere of influence. God is the entrusted of all of these.

God expects you to manage what He has entrusted to you with faithfulness, accountability, wisdom, righteousness and responsibility. The scriptures tell us that if we are faithful over the little, God will make us ruler over the much.

The concept of stewardship is rooted in being trustworthy in the little things. This is an antecedent to being entrusted with greater duty and compensation. The Bible emphasizes that if a person can be trusted in small things, their responsible character speaks for them that they can handle larger duties.

A CROWN OF BEAUTY FOR ASHES

The concept of stewardship is also rooted in honesty. Honesty is having principled integrity and consistency in your acts, conduct, and behavior. Matthew 25:21: This passage tells the parable of the talents, where a master admires a servant who was faithful with a few talents, saying, "Well done, good and faithful servant. You have been faithful over a little; I will set you over much. Enter the joy of your master".

This demonstrates that faithful stewardship in small matters is rewarded with more power and duties because of your good judgement.

The stewardship belief places attention on the concept that little actions of genuineness contribute to constructing a foundation for greater things. Whether it's being responsible with a small finance, thoroughly completing small everyday jobs, or being dependable in prayer and other spiritual observances; these apparently small acts reveal a character that is worthy of trust and capable of managing more.

Another element of stewardship that is critical to your healing, restoration, multiplication and success is carefully being a good manager of your body, the Temple of God. Keeping your temple spiritually clean/Holy and healthy makes you feel good about yourself.

As a believer your body is God' house; out of respect you should honor God with your body. 1 Peter 1:18 states for you know that God paid a ransom to save you from the empty life you inherited from your ancestors. And it was not paid with merely gold or silver, which loses their value.

A CROWN OF BEAUTY FOR ASHES

Jesus Christ's Blood paid for your freedom; you no longer must be a slave of sin and filth. Considering this powerful and victorious truth, you do not have to struggle to use your body to glorify God. Your behavior, consumptions, deeds, speech, and thoughts should worship and reverence God; and be a testament of stewardship.

What you allow into your temple through your mouth, ears, eyes and intimate encounters should be censored through the word of God, for everything that we do He sees.

 Acknowledging and accepting your body to be a sacred place keeps you in alignment with living by the Spirit and dead to gratifying the desire of the sinful nature and forbidden things that leads to death.

 Understanding stewardship is also rooted in realizing that God owns everything. Psalm 24:1 states, "The earth is the Lord's, and all it contains, the world, and those who dwell in it." God has power over everyone and everything, we are responsible to take care of what He has created. Being a good steward is about thoughtfully considering that God is the landlord of all things, and we are to manage what He has given us for his purpose and glory.

Good stewards do not live to be controlling tyrants, they desire to live as servants, and their service is a commitment that involves wise management.

Assignment: Journal the ways you can be a good steward over what God has given you to manage.

Day 30

Keep Looking in the Mirror

"Anyone who listens to the word but does not do what it says is like someone who looks at his face in a mirror and, after looking at himself, goes away and immediately forgets what he looks like." – James 1:23-24.

The word of God is the mirror that you should be looking in 24/7. The word of God shows you what you look like and what you should look like. A person looks into a physical mirror to examine their physical appearance to identify what needs to be changed or adjusted. When you read and study the perfect law of liberty, it shows you spiritual changes and adjustments that are needed. When you study God's word daily, it should be a time of self-inspection as measured by God's standard of expectation.

 Looking into the mirror of God's word should not be an unintentional glance. This must be an intentional act. Reading the word of God requires a candid reflection of what is being revealed unto you as you read it. Reading the word of God requires more than a quick peep. You must study to inspect your heart and life in the light of God's Word. This involves time, attention, and genuine commitment.

 Do you want good success to accompany your healing, restoration and multiplication? Joshua 1:8 reads, "Keep this Book of the Law always on your lips; meditate on it day and night, so that you may be careful to do everything written in it. Then you will be prosperous and have good success."

Assignment: What change(s) did you make in your life today after looking into the mirror of God's word?

Day 31
Live Positive

Decide to live with a positive mindset every day. The word positive means constructive, optimistic, or confident. Decree and declare that today and everyday your life will be filled with helpful, beneficial, cheerful, and assured communication.

Life happens to all of us. We all have experienced some traumatic experience(s). We have all experienced some ups and some downs. Not many people get through life without being scared or scratched. Even if you could not prevent what happened to you, you can live beyond regret and prevent negativity from becoming the default of your mindset   So, let's establish some healthy habits to stay positive.

1.   Focus on the good

2.   Limit social media

3.   Smile more- frownless

4.   Use positive words

5.   Have a regular exercise routine

6.   Be mindful about who you are spending your time with

7.   Eat healthy

8.   Remember having a hobby(ies) is fun enjoyment

Assignment: call a friend to share these 8 healthy habits for positive living.   Make a list of positive words and statements you will speak for the next 31 days.

You Made It

You just increased your value.

You made it.   My prayer is that you will start over again and read through this devotional for the next 31 days again.

How did you increase your value? You increased your value by completing your goal of reading this devotional. You finished what you started. The reward is in finishing what is started. The race is not given to the swift nor the battle to the strong but to the one who endures to the end.

You have increased your value because you have gained wisdom. The Bible says that a wise woman builds her house, but a foolish woman tears her house down. Knowledge and wisdom go hand in hand. During this 31-day journey prayerfully you have gained more knowledge and insight from God's word.

 Gaining knowledge is transformative. Through the understandings gleaned from the scriptures, you are fortified and invigorated to grow, develop and progress. This involves releasing and departing from old ways and patterns and embracing the new paths God is desiring for you to travel. Transformation is easy when you make the decision to let go of everything that is hindering your true progress.

 Jesus encouraged Peter that after his conversion to strengthen the brethren/sisters. No person can truly offer the help, support, and guidance on another's journey if he or she have not been converted. Converted means having been adapted (changed, altered, revised) to be suitable (appropriate) for a new purpose. It is when you understand your spiritual value you can reflect Christ in your home, community and the world.

In conclusion, we acknowledge that the Bible/sacred writings are the primary source of all knowledge. It is through God's Word that we come to know His character and His will for our lives. As you submerse yourself in Scripture, you discover truths that guide, test, challenge and encourage. The knowledge found in the Bible prepares you to handle the uncertainties of life and share God's love with others. May you always select His Word in your pursuit for knowledge.

Assignment: Begin reading this devotion again. The word of God is spiritual food. Do you remember what you ate 31 days ago? If your answer is no, begin from day 1 to continue feasting on the word of God.

Conclusion
The Importance of Prayer and Fasting

Jesus said that He gave you the keys of the Kingdom and whatever you bind on Earth shall be bound in heaven and whatever you lose on Earth shall be loosed in heaven.

Jesus has given authority to those whom eyes have been opened to the fullness of who Christ is. To these He has given the authority to **"bind and loose,"** meaning to declare what is forbidden or permitted, but always in alignment with God's will, unlocking access to salvation and spiritual blessings. This is why it is so important to know the word of God and your inheritance in the word. Once individuals know their spiritual inheritance, they know what to permit (allow) in their life and what to forbid.

The BLOOD OF JESUS Is another weapon of prayer. When you apply through faith the BLOOD OF JESUS over every area of your life and your family, you are decreeing the most effective and powerful spiritual weapon for triumphant victories, all-inclusive protection, deliverance from sin and evil, and cleansing from the immoral filth and the stain of sin. The BLOOD OF JESUS allows you to overcome spiritual and physical maladies and activate God's covenant promises over your entire life. Declare the BLOOD of JESUS washes away all fear.

In addition, as the end times are upon us, **prayers releasing the fire of God** will be a necessary warfare weapon for purification, protection and destruction of the works of darkness. Zechariah 2:5 (KJV/ESV),: "For I, saith the LORD, will be unto her a wall of fire round about, and will be the glory in the midst of her." God is the only sources of divine protection, the most powerful defender, and He takes delight in surrounding his people with his presence. Fire is a manifestation of God's penetrating unbearable holiness, glory, power and judgement. The God you serve is a consuming fire. God is the God who answers by fire. Fire burns away evil influences. His glory eradicates evil and sin. **The LORD'S prayer** is a model prayer that Jesus taught his disciples to pray. "Our Father, who art in heaven, hallowed be thy name; thy kingdom come; thy will be done; on earth as it is in heaven. Give us this day our daily bread. And forgive us our trespasses, as we forgive those who trespass against us. And lead us not into temptation; but deliver us from evil, for Thine is the Kingdom, the Power, and the Glory forever- Amen.

Fasting for the believer is an understood expectation. Fasting involves more than abstaining from food and drink The phrase "If you do not fast from the world, you will not find the kingdom" comes from Saying 27 of the Gospel of Thomas. You will discover who Christ is and receive the benefits of salvation when you disconnect from worldly desires, worldly preoccupations and the material concerns. This is the way that the Kingdom of God within will be known and manifested. By fasting (food, drink and from the world) you are making your spiritual focus a priority over the flesh- worldly passions and desires.

John Chapter 17 Amplified [13] But now I am coming to You; and I say these things [while I am still] in the world so that they may experience My joy made full and complete and perfect within them [filling their hearts with My delight]. [14] I have given to them Your word [the message You gave Me]; and the world has hated them because they are not of the world and do not belong to the world, just as I am not of the world and do not belong to it. [15] I do not ask You to take them out of the world, but that You keep them and protect them from the evil one. [16] They are not of the world, just as I am not of the world. [17] Sanctify them in the truth [set them apart for Your purposes, make them holy]; Your word is truth. [18] Just as You commissioned and sent Me into the world, I also have commissioned and sent them

(believers) into the world. [19] For their sake [e]I sanctify Myself [to do Your will], so that they also may be sanctified [set apart, dedicated, made holy] in [Your] truth.

1 Peter chapter 2 Amplified   Beloved, I
urge you as aliens and strangers [in this
world] to abstain from the sensual urges
[those dishonorable desires] that wage
war against the soul.

The Book of Philip Vs. 105

105. Not all who have a body are able to cognize their own Essence. And those who cannot cognize their own Essence cannot use the possibilities given to them for enjoyment. Only those who cognized their own Essence will enjoy truly. To cognize the highest enjoyment, one has to make great efforts on self-development. Only the one who succeeds in the cognition of the Father attains this. The cognition of one's own Essence is the realization of oneself as a

Consciousness in the Abode of the Father. He is our Higher Self, which is cognized when we infuse ourselves into Him.

Supernatural recovery, restoration and multiplication belongs to you!

Know who you are in God/Christ.

Thank you and may God richly bless you.